Introduction

'That was what I wanted to ask you', said Pooh, 'because my spelling is wobbly. It's good spelling but it Wobbles and the letters get in the wrong places.'

A A Milne *Winnie the Pooh* 1926

Given time and understanding, we hope that all children will approach the task of writing uninhibited by a temporary wobble in their spelling.

Spelling development

Interest and research into the nature of children's writing and spelling abilities have revealed that young writers move through clearly recognisable stages which parallel earlier language developments.

The existence of these stages suggests that learning to spell is developmental and not merely a matter of memorising words. It is associated with developing cognitive strategies and linguistic growth.

This developmental, cognitive view of spelling accommodates all spellers, whether they are good, bad or anything in between. In teaching spelling, it is therefore necessary to understand these developmental stages, to identify which stage each child has reached, and then to promote progress through each stage until spelling competency is achieved.

The main spelling stages are: pre-communicative, semi-phonetic, phonetic, transitional and correct.

The pre-communicative speller

The pre-communicative speller:
• demonstrates some knowledge of the alphabet by writing letters to represent a message;
• has no knowledge of letter-sound correspondence, spelling appears to be a random stringing together of those letters the writer is able to produce;
• may or may not know that English spelling goes from left to right;
• may include numbers as well as letters;
• mixes upper and lower case letters and generally shows a preference for upper case letters;
• writes purposefully – their writing represents their concept of words, but does not communicate language because a speller at this stage is constrained by lack of knowledge of letter-sound correspondence: eg the child might write TX and say that it means 'This is my house'.

The semi-phonetic speller

This type of speller:
• begins to realise that letters have sounds which are used to represent sounds in words;
• abbreviates words – one, two or three letters may be used to represent a whole word;
• uses a letter name instead of a word: eg R=are, U=you;
• is beginning to grasp left to right sequential arrangements of letters;
• has a more complete knowledge of the alphabet and mastery of letter formation;
• may or may not understand and use word segmentation.

The semi-phonetic stage is important, as the speller begins to link letters to sounds: for example, a child writes in all letter shapes, usually with some correspondence: eg MSR=monster, KR=car.

The phonetic speller

The phonetic-stage speller:
- is able to provide a total mapping of letter-sound correspondence – all the surface sound features of the word being spelt are represented in the spelling;
- is systematically developing particular spellings for certain details of phonetic form: eg tense, long/short vowels, pre-consonantal nasals, 'ed' endings;
- assigns letters strictly on a basis of sound – there is no regard for

acceptable letter sequence or other conventions of English orthography;
- generally but not always shows evidence of word segmentation and spatial orientation.

During this stage the spellers are inventive, creating an orthographic system that completely represents the surface sound structure of the words being spelt.

They usually demonstrate a wide variety of written forms, appearing to enjoy using this developing form of communication. Common forms include lists, notices, labels, greeting cards and letters.

With encouragement, and by being allowed to invent spelling, the phonetic-stage speller starts to develop a cognitive awareness of English orthography (later

demonstrated in the correct stage, when the speller says a word 'doesn't look right').

At this stage the child knows and tries to represent words: eg MOSTR=monster and ATE=eighty.

The transitional-stage speller

At this stage the speller:
- adheres to basic conventions of English orthography;
- uses vowels in every syllable;
- represents nasals before consonants;
- is developing visual and formation strategies: eg EIGHTEE rather than ATE=80;
- may reverse some letters in words due to developing visual strategy: eg HUOSE=HOUSE;

- uses learned words (ie correctly spelt words) in greater abundance.

During this stage, the speller begins to assimilate the conventional alternatives for representing sounds.

The transitional stage marks a speller's movement away from reliance on sound representing words towards a greater reliance on the visual and the formation of words.

When the speller reaches this stage, spelling instruction helps to consolidate knowledge and promote spelling competency.

The correct-stage speller
By now the speller:
- has a basic knowledge of the English orthographic system and its basic rules;

- has a knowledge of word structure – prefixes, suffixes, contractions and compound words;
- has an ability to distinguish homonyms;
- has a growing accuracy in the use of silent and double consonants;
- is able to think of alternative spellings and uses visual strategies for misspelt words: eg they will say 'It doesn't look right';
- continues to master alternative uncommon patterns (eg ie/ei) and irregular spellings;
- masters Latinate forms and other morphological structures;
- accumulates a large spelling vocabulary of learned words.

In the context of developmental spelling, the term 'correct' does not mean the ability to spell every word correctly. Rather it means that correct spelling may exist at different levels:

ie correct spelling is possible at eight or eleven years of age, but there are different levels, depending upon maturity, extent of vocabulary, etc.

The correct spelling stage therefore represents a position at which the speller's basic knowledge is firmly fixed and from which more formal and systematic spelling instruction can be useful and productive.

A chart showing Gentry's (1981) spelling stages is given on page 8.

Types of speller
As we do not know exactly how children learn, we cannot say that any one method or approach can be used to teach all children to spell. However, teachers need to be aware of the different teaching methods available so that they may decide how best to help each child in their class.

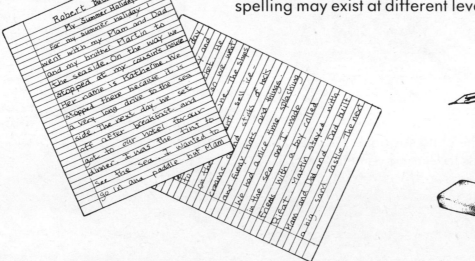

When children start school many of them have already picked up ideas about writing and spelling. They have heard and seen language used; some will have already thought about words and observed that certain symbols represent words or parts of words: for example, the name of the shop displayed above such stores as Tesco are often recognised by pre-school children if their parents shop there, even when seen in a different locality. Some children even notice the letter differences and say 'What does that mean?' pointing out the O. They are already absorbing visual clues.

Others chant phrases like 'p-p-pick up a Penguin' and have begun to associate sounds with symbols.

While many children will continue to learn by absorbing their environment others will need help at various stages in their development.

The bizarre speller or dyslexic child

There is considerable controversy over the term 'dyslexia'. It is sometimes called specific learning difficulties or word blindness.

The fact is that there are people who find it almost impossible to master conventional spelling. It looks as though these spellers are 'stuck' in the pre-phonetic development stage (see chart on page 8).

They frequently use letter names to represent whole or parts of words: for example, say=SA. They reverse many letters for far longer than expected, especially those that are mirror images: for example, db. Their writing appears almost totally unreadable: for example, one child wrote 'Ob not boop' meaning 'Do not smoke'.

It is a condition that causes anxiety and distress to the child and parents, and represents a daunting task to the classroom teacher. There is no easy way for these children to become proficient spellers.

However, recognition of the undoubted effort that they expend to produce any piece of writing, coupled with an understanding of spelling development can relieve the situation.

A practical and structured approach has been offered by Dr B Hornsby in the publication *Alpha to Omega*, requiring a one-to-one teaching situation. Dr Lynette Bradley has also developed the following method:

● The child suggests the word he wants to learn. Even if the word appears far too difficult, it reflects his interests and vocabulary.
● The word is either made from plastic script letters (which the child can handle and move around independently) or written down.
● The child names the word.
● He then writes the word saying the alphabetic name of each letter as it is written.
● He says the word again and checks to see that it is correct.
● He repeats the above steps twice more until he can manage without the stimulus word.
● He practises this word every day for six days. Be careful this does not deteriorate into rote spelling.
● The child is then encouraged to generalise from this word to words with similar sounds and orthographic patterns using the plastic script letters.

Bradley suggests that the whole procedure should be done consistently for one week.

The unexpected poor speller

Some children appear to have no reading problems but are severely handicapped with their spelling.

Dr Uta Frith called these 'unexpected poor spellers'. She found that this type of child seems to use two different strategies for reading and spelling. They learn to read 'by eye' but they write 'by ear'. This implies that they have 'stuck' at the phonic stage.

Whereas the good speller retains

the visual image of the word, the unexpected poor speller relies heavily on sounds. These children need to develop visual strategies.

The majority of spellers

Dr Margaret Peters carefully examined children who seemed to have no spelling problems. They appear to use similar strategies – they take an interest in words and retain a good visual image of the word. When in doubt, they try writing down possible alternatives and then say 'That doesn't look right.'

To foster good spelling Dr Peters advises teachers to be consistent:

interest the children in words, find root words or words within words, seek out connections between words, collect word families and pay attention to letter clusters. Above all, children should be taught a strategy for getting spelling right.

The 'look, cover, write and check' approach has been found helpful to children, enabling them to become confident, competent spellers.

Look, cover, write and check

First, the child must look at the word until she feels she can reproduce it. Next she covers up the word and, if possible, writes it in fast-flowing

handwriting. Finally, she checks the word against the original.

Teachers should aim to encourage an interest in words, a delight in language and a desire to use it, coupled with confident spelling strategies. The more children write, the more opportunities they have both to extend vocabulary and to develop spelling ability.

'There will always be errors in word detail if the child is motivated to express his ideas, rather than merely stay within the confines of the vocabulary with which he is familiar and the skills he can control.' Marie Clay, *What Did I Write?*

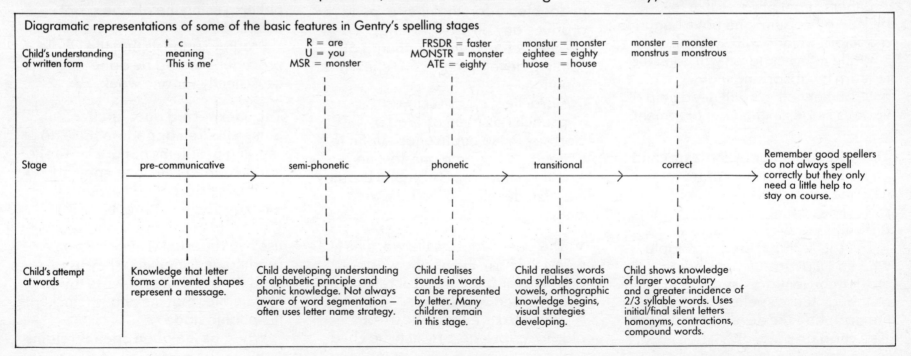

Diagramatic representations of some of the basic features in Gentry's spelling stages

Child's understanding of written form	t c meaning 'This is me'	R = are U = you MSR = monster	FRSDR = faster MONSTR = monster ATE = eighty	monstur = monster eightee = eighty huose = house	monster = monster monstrus = monstrous
Stage	pre-communicative	semi-phonetic	phonetic	transitional	correct	Remember good spellers do not always spell correctly but they only need a little help to stay on course.
Child's attempt at words	Knowledge that letter forms or invented shapes represent a message.	Child developing understanding of alphabetic principle and phonic knowledge. Not always aware of word segmentation – often uses letter name strategy.	Child realises sounds in words can be represented by letter. Many children remain in this stage.	Child realises words and syllables contain vowels, orthographic knowledge begins, visual strategies developing.	Child shows knowledge of larger vocabulary and a greater incidence of 2/3 syllable words. Uses initial/final silent letters homonyms, contractions, compound words.

Spelling chart

Game	SEMI-PHONETIC	PHONETIC	TRANSITIONAL	CORRECT
Alphabet mat	X	x	X	x
Alphabet sequence games		X	X	X
Blend and build	X	X	X	
Bright sight	X	X		X
Burglar Bill		X		
Clear the board	X	X		X
Cup cap game	X	X	X	
Dragon snap	x	X	X	X
Escape	X	X	X	
Feel and say		X	X	X
Hide and seek	X	X	X	X
Justification pairs		X	X	X
Kim's game		X	X	X
King patience		X	X	X
Lucky dip	X	X	X	X
Noughts and crosses		X	X	
Omega trail	X	X	X	X
Roots	x		X	X
Self check	x	X	X	X
Silent bingo		X	X	X
Spellasaurus		X		
Spelling dominoes		X		X
Split	X			
Spot the ladybird	X	X		X
Take one, make one			X	
Think and link			X	X
Three in a bed		X	X	X
Traffic lights			X	
What is it?	X	X	X	
Word clock patience	X	X	X	

Spelling questions and answers

Is there a place for formal spelling instruction?

Formal instruction should take place in the classroom, but before this can be effective you need to establish which developmental stage the child has reached (see diagram on page 8).

Instruction can take place with individual children or in groups, and it has been found more effective to spend a few minutes every day rather than an hour every week. At all times, it should be a shared, interesting, enjoyable activity, giving everyone involved an opportunity to contribute (see 'Spelling activities' on page 50).

Spelling tests are a good idea if a group of children are at the same stage of spelling development and are persistently making the same mistakes. After discussion with the group a joint list to be learned and tested could be drawn up.

However, you should not use a spelling list which has been abstracted from a published list, since it is highly unlikely to be of use to most of the class. Also, lists should not be used regularly, but only to meet a particular need – for example, to provide unusual words related to a project.

If it is obvious that the child is under stress, then no testing should take place until the teacher is sure that the child's anxiety has disappeared. It is not unknown for children who are submitted to weekly class spelling tests, in which they are sure they will fail, to become even poorer spellers.

11

What are the limitations of testing?

The following limitations should be taken into consideration if a standardised test is administered:

• The test vocabulary may bear no relationship to the words the child/children are using.

• The marking only allows for right or wrong. One child might spell 'because' as 'becos', while another might write 'dacus'; the test makes no allowances for the obvious difference between these two spellings – both are wrong but the first child is further on the way to getting the word right.

• The tests are generally dictated single words rather than continuous prose. In continuous writing, children are more likely to spell automatically, not worrying over possible alternatives; in a word list, each word becomes a test.

• Spelling tests are usually converted into a spelling age, or spelling quotient. To learn that a child entering your class has a spelling age of 7.6 gives you no indication of his developmental stage, or how he could be helped to raise this figure; it only tells you how he compares with his peers.

• The word 'test' causes anxiety, especially to the child who considers herself unable to spell; this may further depress what is likely to be a low score. Additionally, some children who are good spellers often doubt their original spelling choice, crossing out the correct spelling in favour of an incorrect one (eg 'library' becomes 'liberary', 'Britain' become 'Britian').

Note: If the teacher is under pressure, or feels it is necessary to test children, it is more useful to dictate a piece of continuous prose.

Should I teach spelling rules?

Teaching rules and recognising patterns is only relevant to children in the transitional and correct stages of spelling development.

There are very few spelling rules, but there are many letter patterns. The children must understand these patterns before they can easily accept the exceptions.

For example: the rule 'i before e except after c when the sound is e' works in all cases, but children rarely understand the second part of this rule. One child was influenced to spell the word 'eight' as 'ieght'; he had spelt this correctly for many years but on being given the mnemonic and observing that there was no 'c' present, he changed the spelling and then felt let down by the rule and became a less confident speller for some time.

Do not confuse the children by offering alternative or slightly differing letter-strings at the same time: for example, ei/ie ceiling/piece.

i before e except after c ceiling receive

How do I evaluate and mark spelling?

Evaluating children's spelling is obviously open to misinterpretation. It is very difficult to be certain about the cause of an error, which could be due to a number of reasons:

- a slip of the pen,
- a misinterpretation of poor handwriting by the teacher,
- reliance on poor spoken grammar (eg 'must of'),
- reversal of letters (eg 'bd'),
- slight reversal of letters (eg 'throuhg'),
- a confusion over the meaning of two similar words (eg 'there' 'their').

If these errors are highlighted by over-marking, it often gives a wrong impression of a child's spelling ability.

It is obviously damaging for a child to receive back a piece of work that is 'overly corrected', or in which every mistake has been identified.

Marking will depend very much on how important it is to have correct spelling. If the work is a final draft before writing in 'best', the child and the teacher will want to provide a perfectly spelt piece of work. If it is a piece of regular classwork then it will entirely depend on the teacher's discretion and classroom practice.

Marking should ideally be done with the child. Teacher and child can then identify the errors together, correct the spellings and discuss any handwriting improvements or difficulties. It may even be possible to produce a typed version or a computer print-out.

Finally, the teacher should recognise and evaluate the effort the child has made: ie have a positive approach, which may include criticism where necessary, but should contain as much praise as possible.

The following headings could be used as a basis for charting the child's efforts in all aspects ot writing:

Child's name: Sylvia **Title:** The Viking Chief

Date	Effort	Content	Expression	Spelling	Presentation
1.1.90	good	interesting	fluent	11 errors	weak – no margin, poor letter formation.

Interpretation: This child writes with ease. She has no real problem with content, grammar or spelling but she needs to take more pride in her final presentation. She uses language adventurously, hence her 11 errors.

Child's name: Diana **Title:** The Viking Ships

Date	Effort	Content	Expression	Spelling	Presentation
1.1.90	good	poor	v weak v limited vocab	3 errors (only uses known words)	very neat careful

Interpretation: This child needs encouragement to experiment with language. She tries hard and spends many hours producing a beautiful piece of work but which is very limited in content and language.

How do I measure spelling progress?

Most teachers have found that success in the class spelling test is not reflected in other writing activities.

One of the simplest ways of monitoring a child's progress is to compare pieces of writing over a period of time. By discussing the pieces together, the child and teacher can both recognise improvement, which often gives the child pleasure and pride in his developing abilities.

A useful practice for the child at the transitional stage, which enables him to write fluently without fear of spelling errors, is to encourage him to leave gaps for the doubtful words (or to put the first letter only followed by a gap). The teacher is then able to provide the missing word. If this is written in pencil in the margin, when the child has finished writing he can use the 'look, cover, write, check' technique to fill in the gaps.

Note: It is useful to have margins on either side of the page, so that a left-handed writer has words written in the right-hand margin, and vice versa.

Is there a basic checklist?

When teachers are attempting to assess a child's spelling progress, they will find it cannot be measured by an improvement in spelling alone especially if the teacher is hoping to see a reduction in the total number of errors in the child's free writing. As children develop, their vocabulary also increases, so that it is conceivable that they could be making progress and yet still be writing the same percentage of errors. The difference would be in the vocabulary and not in the number of words misspelt.

The following checklist is only a suggested guide for teachers; it is hoped that teachers will extend and develop it according to their priorities.

- Can the child form all her lower case letters correctly?
- Can the child form all his upper case letters correctly?
- Does he know the alphabetic names for every letter?
- What is the child's attitude to writing – enthusiastic, conforming, diffident or reluctant?
- Is the child only writing words that he can spell?
- Is the child overly concerned about spelling: ie does she spend more time rubbing out than is necessary?
- Is the child aware of her spelling mistakes? Does she 'see' when a word 'doesn't look right'?
- If this is the case, has she progressed to being able to offer a solution?
- Has he moved towards 'look, cover, write, check', and does he use it as a natural approach?
- Has she begun to use a dictionary?

Should I involve parents?

Parents often say: 'My son/daughter's spelling is awful!' They are usually speaking from a position of a competent speller, and do not remember or consider how long it took them to reach this stage. To them, unconventional and invented spelling needs attention.

It is not always easy to convince parents that you, as a teacher, are teaching spelling if there is no weekly spelling test and their child's book is not comprehensively marked for spelling mistakes.

The following suggestions will help you to encourage parental help and understanding:

• Explain to parents the stages of spelling development, and the school's attitude and policy. Just as they can accept the developmental nature of growth (eg in mobility and speech), so they can quite easily accept the same kind of development in spelling and reading.

• Show the parents their children's writing and how it has progressed. It is useful if a parent can identify a mistake and then see how long it takes for this to become corrected. This should not be a criticism but an encouragement for the child's writing efforts, primarily looking for the meaning in his work, and incidentally helping with his spelling.

• Invite the parents to your classroom to see your spelling policy in action. Soon you might persuade them to come and play some of the spelling games with small groups.

• Send home activities. Many parents want to help their child but are worried about 'doing the wrong thing'. If the parent wishes to help the child with spelling, explain the need for the child to see the word written down correctly by them, and the 'look, cover, write, check' technique. Many of the games and activities in this book could be sent home for them to do.

A photocopy of do's and don'ts for parents can be found on page 109.

Does the computer help with spelling?

The computer is undoubtedly a challenging and exciting teaching aid, as long as the programs are carefully evaluated. The teacher must be sure that they meet the

spelling needs of the children and that they complement the spelling policy.

Children can be persuaded to sit for a long time in front of a busy, active screen, but could be learning very little. It is possible that some programs could weaken the skills that the child has already acquired by, for example, requiring them to copy letter by letter instead of encouraging them to recall letter-strings or whole words.

Is there a link between handwriting and spelling?

Dr Margaret Peters found that good spellers are more likely to have good joined handwriting than poor spellers. Whether this is because they can spell and are therefore released from stopping in the middle of words to think how they are spelt, or whether they are taught a good basic handwriting style, ensuring that they do not stop to think and therefore reinforcing correct spelling, we do not know.

However, the visual presentation of a piece of written work becomes increasingly more important to the child, teacher and parent as the child gets older.

A useful and enjoyable exercise is to use a triple-line book. Select the letter-string and then find several words containing that string. The teacher writes the word down the left-hand side of a double-page spread, then the child writes across both pages, practising the letter-shape and handwriting. For example:

knit knit   knit knit
knitting
knees
knock

Finally, the child turns over the page and covers the previous writing. She writes the word on the new page, then slides the page back and checks the spelling against the teacher's original.

Note: For this activity, always use a pencil. It grips the paper and the child gets much more feel of the movement.

Do writing implements aid spelling?

The choice of writing implement can affect a child's writing. If his writing is very small, a fine point helps to clarify the letters. (He may be writing very small to disguise his spelling!)

If a child writes exceptionally large letters, a fat point tends to make them appear more balanced.

If a child appears to have difficulty controlling the writing implement, holding a fatter barrel will give him more motor control.

Most children, but especially younger pupils, like using highlighter pens. Generally, these are used to enhance a word that has already been written, but this can be done the other way round.

Young children, when beginning to write, often become bogged down, not only because of the spellings, but also

Last night I watched cartoons on television. They were really good

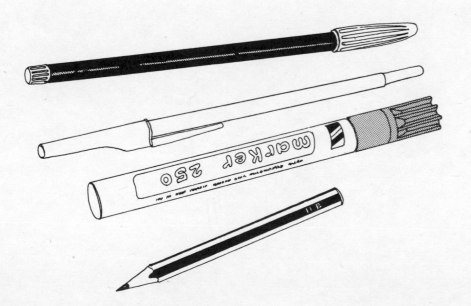

in remembering how to make the letter shapes. The teacher can help by using a highlighter pen to write the child's dictated sentence. Then the child goes over this writing using a pencil.

Letter shape and correct spelling are both encouraged by this method, and the result is highly satisfying, as the child's own letters appear to be highlighted.

Copying underneath a teacher's written sentences tends to emphasise how much 'worse' the child is than the teacher, but highlighting has a more positive effect.

The teacher could also write in large clear print the words the child wants, and then the child can highlight these by tracing over them with a highlighter pen. It is certainly more satisfactory than using tracing paper, which always appears to have a will of its own!

Spelling games

Alphabet mat

Spelling aims
To get children to create words from randomly selected letters and to encourage word building.

Spelling stage
Transitional; with variation, phonetic and correct.

Number of players
Two to six.

What you need
1 sheet of A3 card,
1 coin or rolling counter or spinning top,
1 set of duplicated letters or cut squares of paper on which to write letters for each player.

How to make
Divide the sheet into 36 squares, 6 × 6. Clearly write letters in lower case as follows:
1 × every consonant,
2 × every vowel,
1 × sp, 1 × th, 1 × ch, 1 × br, 1 × sh.

How to play
The object is to create as many correctly spelt words as possible from the letters received.

Players take it in turns to roll a coin on the board, then each receives a duplicate of the letter the coin settled on.

Each player collects a previously agreed number of letters, then has three minutes or one egg-timer allowance in which to write down as many words as possible from his selection on to a sheet of paper.

One point is allocated for each letter in any word spelt

correctly. (Note: Only one mark is given for each blend or digraph already given on the board.)

The winner is the player who has the highest score after a set number of games or the first player to reach a score of 25.

Variation
● Put common letter-strings into each square. Players have to make words which include that letter-string.
Note: It is easier for players to have a separate piece of card for each letter, as this leads to more experimentation.

Alphabet sequence games

Spelling aim
To encourage familiarity and fluency with alphabet order.

Spelling stage
With variations, suitable for all stages.

Number of players
Two to four.

What you need
52 plain playing cards, card, coloured pens.

How to make
Make two complete lower case alphabets, one letter per card, and each alphabet in a different colour (see photocopy master pages 120 to 123).

How to play
Deal seven cards to each player and place the remaining cards in a central pool, face downwards.

The first player to identify an 'a' in their hand may start by placing the card face up on the table. If no player has an 'a', then the next letter nearest to 'a' is used to start the play. This player may continue to place the cards in sequence if he is able (ie b, c, d . . .). When his turn is over, he replaces the cards he has played by taking the correct number from the central pool (ie each player should have seven cards after his turn until they run out).

The play moves round clockwise. The second player must do one of the following:
• continue the sequence with one or more cards,
• start a new alphabet if he has an 'a',
• if he has no cards that he can play, he may discard up to three and replace them from the pool; his discarded cards go beneath the pool.

This action constitutes his 'go'.

Play continues until both alphabets are complete. A player may not miss a turn, although he need not play all possible cards.

The last person to play a card loses a life. Three lives lost means the player is out of the game.

Variations
• Start at different letters of the alphabet. This makes the players think about the last letter: for example, if 'm' commences, they have to work out that they must discard the 'l' if possible.
• Play in a circular fashion. Players may go backwards or forwards from the starting letter.
• Hold team races with two players per team. The alphabets need to be sorted according to their colour for this game. The first team to put down the alphabet correctly wins.
• When playing individually, children may use a stop-watch to time how long it takes to lay out the alphabet.
• An upper case alphabet could be made and either replace one of the lower case alphabets or be a third set to use as in the original game.

Blend and build

Spelling aim
To encourage building words beginning with a blend.

Spelling stage
Phonetic.

Number of players
Two to four.

What you need
Copy page 77, card, 48 plain playing cards.

How to make
Make a copy of the sheet on page 77 for each player. It is advisable to mount this on good card and laminate it if possible.

Make 48 word-ending cards (see page 75), then choose six initial blends and write each twice on to blank squares in the grid.

How to play
Each player is given a copy of the playing sheet. The word-ending cards are shuffled and placed face down in a central pile.

Players take it in turns to pick up a card. If a player can make a word, he places it on a lined square next to the correct blend. (Note: He may now verify this word by referring to the checklist given on page 77.) If he cannot make a word, he replaces the card under the pile face down.

Play continues until one player has completed his board.

br		br	ick
cr	isp	cr	
fl		fl	
fr	og	bl	
bl		fl	
fl		fr	

Variations
• The following pairs of blends could be given as they sort out confusion between similar initial sounds: cl, gl; dr, tr; pl, bl.
• The following pairs of blends could be used: pr, br; cr, gr; fl, fr.
• The following pairs of blends could be used: sl, st; sp, sw; sn, sm.
• Use an extra set of endings to match the three-letter blends, as they are more limited: scr, spl, spr, squ, str. See the checklist on page 76. Remove endings that provide nonsense words for this game.
Note: All these blends have been matched with clear phonetic endings. They may be used with vowel digraphs, final endings, etc.
• This game can also be played using a 'lucky dip' bag (see page 32).

Bright sight

Spelling aims
To encourage children to look at, search and identify letters and to ensure correct letter formation.

Spelling stage
Semi-phonetic.

Number of players
Two to four.

What you need
Sheet of paper and highlighter pens for each child, cards.

How to make
Write on a sheet of paper the letters you would like the children to practise. The number of letters could range between one and five.

Make large call cards, each showing one letter.

How to play
Give each child a sheet of paper with the letters written on, then choose a letter call-card and display this to the players.

Each player looks at the card and then identifies the letter, if it is on their sheet of paper, by marking a dot under the letter. You then put the call-card face down on the table.

The players take it in turns to highlight the letter by tracing over it using the correct letter formation.

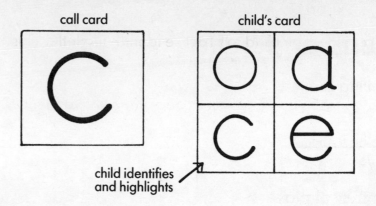

call card   child's card

child identifies and highlights

The winner is the player who highlights all his letters first.

Note: Do not put easily reversed or very similar letters on the same sheet in the early stages of this game, such as: db, ij, mw, un, etc.

Variations
• You can use the same game to identify and trace over two-letter clusters, such as: bl, cl, th.

call card   child's card

• This can be increased up to five letters according to the maturity of the players.

- It can also be used to practise identifying letter clusters in the initial, medial and final position within words.

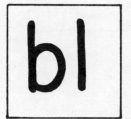

bl	dl	pl
lb	ld	bl

blanket
plumb
able
constable

Note: Do ensure the player is writing the letters correctly.

Burglar Bill

Spelling aims
To identify, recognise and collect letter families.

Spelling stage
Transitional; with variation, correct.

Number of players
Three to six, but four or more is advisable.

What you need
Cards, one counter for each player (it is better to use small cubes rather than flat counters, as they are easier to steal).

How to make
Each player needs a set of four cards.

Decide on a letter-string for each set: for example, silent b, silent k, silent w (see list on page 78). Write the word in large print in the centre of the card, and in small print in the top left-hand corner.

How to play
The object is to collect a set of four cards and then 'steal' a counter from the table. The player without a counter has to sit out and one set of cards is removed so that there will always be only four cards per player.

Place all the cards face up on the table, and let the players identify letter families before starting the game. Then shuffle the cards and deal them out to each player.

The players study the cards and select which card to discard and which family to collect.

In the centre of the table a counter is placed for each player except one. The caller (either you or a child) says 'pass' and all the players pass their selected card to the player on their left, and pick up a card from the player on their right.

This action continues until one player has a set — she then tries to remove a counter as surreptitiously as possible.

As soon as the other players see the 'burglar' trying to get a counter, they also grab for a counter, whether or not they have a complete set in their hand.

The player without a counter becomes the caller and the game continues until one child is left the winner. Note: It is often necessary to check the sets. If your words are deliberately fairly similar, some players may make mistakes with a set: for example 'where' and 'wrong' were collected in spite of the fact that each player knew they were collecting words with similar first two letters. A general discussion about similarities and differences between the words will help to consolidate the child's awareness and help them to move towards visual recognition of letter patterns rather than sounds.

Variation
● Collecting sets of cards can be varied as much as the teacher wishes, from simple single-letter collecting to fine visual discrimination between 'tion' endings and 'sion' endings.

24

Clear the board

Spelling aim
To get children to give the alphabetic names to letters.

Spelling stage
Semi-phonetic; with variations, phonetic.

Number of players
Two to six.

What you need
Two sheets of card (30cm × 40cm).

How to make
Take a sheet of card, 30cm × 40cm, and divide it into 36 rectangles. On each rectangle write a letter in lower case. Use two rectangles for the d, b, p, m, n, w, j, g, r and f, and one rectangle for every other letter.

Make a corresponding set of cards with a picture for each letter of the alphabet, such as an ant, a bat, a car, and so on. On the reverse put upper case letters, and place the cards over the corresponding letters on the board, picture-side up.

How to play
The object is to collect more cards than the other players. The players take it in turns to choose a card and identify the initial letter by pointing at the picture and saying: 'This is an ant. It begins with a.' If they are correct, they keep the card; if they are incorrect, they replace it.

Variations
• Place the cards letter-side up. Each child chooses a card and writes the lower case letter which matches their choice. She then removes the card and checks underneath. If she is correct, she retains the card; if she is incorrect the card is replaced.
• Players could choose a card and then have to provide another word which begins with the same letter before being allowed to retain the card. (Note: This game really needs an older child or an adult to act as judge.)

The cup cap game

Spelling aim
To get pupils to look carefully at word spellings and to identify the odd word.

Spelling stage
Phonetic; with variations, transitional.

Number of players
Two to six. It is rather a long time between turns with more than six players, but it is possible to play with large groups.

What you need
Basic sheet (see page 80), spinner or die, counters.

How to make
Reproduce the basic sheet on page 80. Decide which words you are going to use, and then write two identical words and one other across each line of the sheet: for example, cup cap cup.

When the sheet is complete, photocopy one copy for each child.

Make a spinner as shown on page 103, or obtain one die, and have a large pool of counters, tiddly-winks or paper squares placed in the centre of the table.

How to play

Give each player a sheet with the words written into each square.

Players take it in turns to throw the die. Each child identifies the number he has thrown and matches it to a row on the sheet. He then takes a counter from the pool in the centre of the table and 'covers' the odd word.

If the child throws a number already covered he cannot go and has to wait for the next turn.

The winner is the first player to cover all six lines correctly.

Note: If unsupervised, some children may take more than one counter and cover two lines in one go! If a supervisor is available it is better to give a counter to the players after each go, rather than let them take counters from the central pile.

Variations

• The level of words chosen by the teacher can be identical for each member of the group, or varying to match each child's personal needs. The words could be chosen from any of the lists on page 79.

• Some children will be tempted to copy their neighbour when covering the odd word. Individual sheets or two variations will prevent this from occurring.

Dragon snap

Spelling aims

To increase the child's awareness of letters and to stimulate recognition of visual discrimination of letter clusters.

Spelling stage

Phonetic; with variations, semi-phonetic.

Number of players

Two, sitting side by side.

What you need

48 plain playing cards.

How to make

Take 48 plain playing cards and mark the top with a notch or a coloured line on the reverse side.

Write the chosen words at the centre of the card in large letters and at the top left-hand side in smaller print. The chosen words can be two-letter matching (dd, db, bb), three-letter words, or blends, ends or medial vowels.

Note: Four copies of each card are recommended to enable a 'snap' situation to occur fairly frequently.

How to play

The object of the game is to 'snap' cards until one player has all the cards.

Shuffle the cards and place them face down on the table. This can be done by the players 'stirring' the cards, as normal shuffling is often too difficult for small hands.

The players take it in turns to pick up one card at a time until all the cards are in their hands. The cards are sorted so that the 'tops' are all at the top. Then they are placed, face down, in front of each player.

The player who sees a 'snap' situation with this pile has to say 'snap dragon'. She may then pick up the card piles which have been 'snapped' and place them under her existing pile.

Variations
• Snap can be played at almost every level. Cards can be made with pictures, letters or the alphabet in upper and lower case. Words of three, four or five letters can be used, or even cards which make a word in either direction: eg was/saw, pin/nip, pot/top, etc.

Escape

Spelling aim
To encourage the 'look, cover, write, check' approach to spelling and to consolidate chosen vocabulary for a topic or to practise own personal spellings.

Spelling stage
Transitional; with variations, phonetic and correct.

Number of players
Two to four.

What you need
Base board (see page 82), card, set of cards, spinner (see page 103) or die, counters.

The players take it in turns to turn over a card. When two identical cards appear the first child to say 'snap' picks up both exposed piles and puts them under his existing pile. Then the game continues.

If 'snap' is said simultaneously, the cards are collected and put (with the last word uppermost) into one pile, so that both players can see the word.

How to make
Reproduce the base board on page 82, stick it on to suitable card and cover it with a transparent seal or laminate.

Devise a set of cards with a specific vocabulary to suit your players and/or topic. Alternatively ask the players to put their own pile of personal spellings face down in front of them.

How to play
The object is to be the first to escape from the 'castle'.

Each player chooses a different-coloured counter and places it in the 'lock-up room'. They must spell a word before they are allowed to move out of the room. The word is chosen by the opponent taking a card from the pile in front of the speller; the opponent names the word and the speller has to write it down on a piece of paper. If she is correct, she may move; if she is incorrect, she has to put the word on the bottom of the pile and try again at the next turn.

The players then take it in turns to throw the die and follow the instructions on the board. If a player lands on a 'spell' square, she has to spell a word correctly (as above) before she can move.

The winner is the first to finish with exactly the correct number thrown.

Feel and say

Spelling aims
To familiarise children with letter shapes through a kinesthetic approach and to link them with letter names.

Spelling stage
Semi-phonetic.

Number of players
One to four, plus adult.

What you need
Plastic letters (available in toy shops in both upper and lower case), large pieces of card.

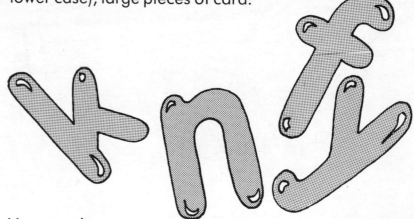

How to play
Ask the child to put his hands behind his back, then give him a plastic letter. He may feel the letter shape for as long as he likes.

Show each child a card on which are written up to six letters, including the one given to the child. Ask the child to identify his letter.

Note: If this is played early in a child's school life, it is a good idea to start with the first letter of the child's name.

Hide and seek

Spelling aim
To encourage children to look at groups of words and to use the 'look, cover, write, check' approach.

Spelling stage
Transitional; with variation, correct.

Number of players
Two to eight.

How to make
Make six flash cards of selected words (related to project work, common mistakes, words with common letter strings or from copy page 83).

How to play
The object is to identify missing words from the group and to write them correctly.

Select one child to be the leader. He lays out all six words so that all the group can clearly see them. The players then close their eyes while the leader removes one card.

The group looks at the remaining cards and then writes down correctly what was on the missing card. The first player to identify and spell the missing word correctly becomes the new leader.

Variation
• Depending on the ability of the group and the difficulty of the cards, players could identify and write down two or more missing words.

Justification pairs

Spelling aims
To encourage careful visual observation of common letter features and to promote logical associations between letters and words.

Spelling stage
Transitional. Depending on the choice of words it is also useful for the 'correct' speller.

Number of players
Two for snap; two to four for pelmanism.

What you need
Plain playing cards (depending on ability and concentration of players you will need between 24 and 48 cards).

How to make
Write words with common features on the cards. You will need at least four cards per letter-string:

eg	
the	one
other	money
mother	telephone
another	tone

How to play
Snap – the object is to collect all the cards.

Divide the cards equally between the players. Each child holds her cards in her hand or keeps them in a pile on the table face down. When a player calls 'snap', she has to justify the reason for claiming the pair. This can be because of a common letter string or even a logical connection: for example, one child connected mother and telephone by saying 'My mother is always on the telephone.'

Note: No single letter matching is allowed.

Pelmanism – the object is to obtain the most pairs.

It is usual to have less cards for pelmanism than for snap, although older children enjoy the challenge of using all the cards.

Place the cards face down on the table. The players take it in turns to turn over any two cards. If they can justify a connection between them, visually, phonically or logically, then they retain them as a pair. If no connection is made then the cards are turned face down again and the next player tries to turn over a justified pair.

Note: No single-letter matching is allowed.

Kim's game

Spelling aims
To memorise words and to use letter-strings.

Spelling stage
Transitional and phonetic; with variations, correct.

Number of players
Two.

What you need
12 plain playing cards,
pencils, paper.

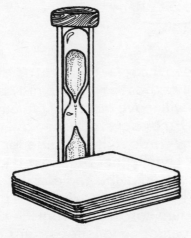

How to make
Divide the cards into two sets of six. Choose two different letter-strings:
eg aw = straw, draw, fawn, claw, awe, dawn.
   or = door, floor, ordinary, score, for, inform.
   Write a word in the centre of each card.

  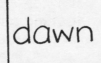

How to play
The object is to remember as many words as possible and write them down correctly.

The players first look at all the cards and identify the letter-strings. They then sort them into the two letter-string groups, one for each player.

Player 1 scrutinises his group for a maximum of three minutes or one run-through of a standard egg-timer.

Player 2 then covers those cards and player 1 endeavours to write down as many words as possible of his letter-string.

When he can remember no more, player 2 exposes the words for him to check. The roles are then reversed and player 2 is given his words to look at.

Each player scores two points for each word remembered and correctly spelt.

You can then play round 2. All the words correctly remembered and spelt in round 1 are removed, and the players begin again with any words incorrectly spelt or forgotten. This time each player gets one point for every correctly spelt word.

For round 3, both players swap cards and start again.

The first player to reach a score of 12 is the winner.
Note: Each player is entitled to the same number of exposures. If both players reach 12 after the same number of goes, the winner is the player with the highest score after the first round.

Variations
● This game could be played using the child's own personal spelling cards (see 'Tips for teachers' on page 70).
● The number of cards can be increased according to ability, but more than 24 makes the game rather long.

King patience

Spelling aim
To aid careful attention to letter-strings in different-sounding words: eg bone, done.

Spelling stage
Transitional; with variation, phonetic and correct.

Number of players
One.

What you need
24 plain playing cards.

How to make
Write a letter-string in red, across the centre and top of four cards: eg ing, old, ay, one. Divide the remaining cards into sets of five. Write different words for each letter-string in black at the centre and top of each card: eg bold, told, fold, cold, scold; bone, done, lone, phone, gone, etc.

How to play
The object is to expose king cards (ie those with red writing) and to build all the other words upon them until all the cards have been used.

Lay five cards on the table – the first four should be face down and the last card upwards. Put a second row of only four cards overlapping the first with the last card face upwards. Continue with three cards, two cards, and one card.

Keep the remaining cards face down in a pile.

Any exposed red king may be placed above the cards. This will leave a card at the end of a row face down which may now be turned over.

Any cards with similar letter-strings may be placed on top of each other or on a red king. If this leaves cards unexposed at the end of a line they may be turned over.

When all the above moves are exhausted, the player may turn cards over from the pile, one at a time. These can be added to letter-strings on the table or, if she exposes a king card, it may be placed above the cards on the table.

The game ceases either when all the cards are exposed and put on the correct king card, or when the cards held in the hand have each been used once.

Variation
● This can be played at most levels: eg using blends, initial letters, medial vowels, etc.

Lucky dip

Spelling aim
To encourage children to build compound words.

Spelling stage
Correct; with variations, semi-phonetic, phonetic and transitional.

Number of players
Two.

What you need
Two bags for children to put their hands in, card.

How to make
The teacher writes a selection of compound words on cards and then cuts them into separate words. The 'beginnings' are put into one bag and the 'endings' into another. See list on page 84.

What to do
This game aims to encourage children to recreate compound words.

The players take it in turns to take cards from each bag until all the cards have been removed. They then make as many compound words as they can from their selection. When both players have finished, they may swap cards to make more words (see page 84 for a selection of compound words).

Each player scores two points for each word made from their selected cards and one point for each word made from a swap. The winner is the player with the highest score.

Variations
This activity could be used for any game that requires pairs of cards: eg homonyms, antonyms, synonyms, initial letter with word end (eg b/at) or just matching as in any 'snap' situation (eg two letters bb/bb).

Noughts and crosses

Spelling aim
To practise personal spelling lists using the 'look, cover, write, check' approach.

Spelling stage
Transitional; with variations, phonetic and correct.

Number of players
Two.

What you need
Board, card for making noughts and crosses or coloured counters, pencils, paper, plain playing cards, envelope for each player.

How to make
Make a traditional noughts and crosses board: ie a square board divided into nine squares. If it is to be used frequently, it is advisable to use good quality card and laminate both sides.

Either make card noughts and crosses (four of each) or allocate two different-coloured counters (four of each).

How to play

The object is to make a diagonal, horizontal or vertical line of one player's counters.

The players swap spelling envelopes which contain personal spellings on cards. Players choose whether they wish to be represented by a nought or a cross (or by a particular colour), then one player selects a spelling from his opponent's envelope, shows it for a few seconds to his opponent and lays it face down on the table.

The opponent endeavours to write this correctly on a rough piece of paper, and both players check for accuracy. If it is correct, she may place her counter, nought or cross in any square.

The second player then selects a word from her opponent's envelope and shows it to him. The opponent tries to write the word correctly, both players check it, and then he may place one of his counters, noughts or crosses, on any vacant square on the board.

The game continues until one player succeeds in completing a line, or until they reach stalemate.

Note: In a class of 30, six boards would be sufficient. Pupils can play this popular game as a practice in spare moments before a final assessment, and children of varying ability could play against each other.

34

Omega trail

Spelling aim
To encourage children to use alphabet names of letters.

Spelling stage
Semi-phonetic; with variations, phonetic.

Number of players
Two to four. (The younger the child, the fewer the players, as young children are less patient awaiting their turn.)

What you need
Base board, counters, die, 12 picture cards, 26 smaller cards.

How to make
Make a base board on as substantial a card as possible. Thin card easily becomes misshapen and the players become frustrated if their markers roll off the board.

Divide the board into 24 squares and number each one in the top right-hand corner. Place a picture card (picture uppermost) on alternate squares. Suggested pictures: apple, bat, cow, dog, egg, fish, gate, hat, ink, jug, king, lemon, mat, net, orange, peg, queen, ring, sun, top, umbrella, van, watch, (fox), yak, zip (see pages 85 and 86).

Make a small card (slightly smaller that the square size) for each letter of the alphabet (except X).

How to play
The object is to get to the last square before the other players.

Each player places a counter on the start. The players take it in turns to throw the die and move their counter the appropriate number of squares.

If a player lands on a card square, he must identify the picture and its initial letter: for example, 'That is a picture of a bat. It begins with the letter b.' If it is confirmed as being correct (either by the supervisor or by the other players), he moves forward three spaces.

This is repeated until one player reaches the finish.

Variations
This game can be played at many developmental levels:
● Players identify initial letter sounds. In this game the card is placed letter side up. The child says 'That letter says b', and turns over the card to check by matching the sound to the initial sound of 'bat'.
● Players identify the final letter by name or sound.
● Players identify the picture, spell the word and then check by turning to the reverse. (The whole word must then be written on the back of the card.)
● Players have to give another word beginning with the same letter.

Roots

Spelling aim
To help children to understand and associate the meanings of common prefixes.

Spelling stage
Correct; with variations, transitional.

Number of players
Two per ten words; maximum of five players.

What you need
Paper for checklist, 20 cards, copy page 87.

How to make
Write a checklist of prefixes and their meanings, then make a set of cards with the prefix on one card and the meaning on another. A maximum of ten pairs is suggested (see list on page 87). Each card pair could be

written in a different colour – this breaks the game into manageable units for learning and sorting.

How to play
Read and discuss the list with the players. Encourage them to provide words which have the prefix chosen: eg anti – antidote, anti-apartheid, anticlockwise.

Give the players the set of cards with the prefixes and meanings and let them sort these into pairs, referring to the checklist.

Once they are familiar with the words, they can play pelmanism. Lay all the cards face down on the table. The players take it in turns to try to pick up pairs. If a matching pair is turned over, they may retain the two cards. If the cards do not make a pair, they are turned face down again. The winner is the player with most pairs.
Note: The checklist should remain on display for reference until all the players have no further need for it.

Consolidation can be achieved through games such as snap or 'Three in a bed' (see page 46).

Variations
Once children are familiar with the complete set of prefixes and meanings, several team games are possible:
• Divide the children into two teams. Give a meaning and ask the teams to write down the corresponding prefix. Each may challenge the opposing team to supply the correct prefix.
• Challenge the teams to find a selected number of words starting with the chosen prefix. In this game, teams may work in consultation. Score the game as follows: one point for a correctly chosen word, one point for explaining the meaning of the word, one point for correctly spelling the word, one point if the word was not offered by any other team.

Self check

Spelling aim
To give practice for personal spelling lists and to use the 'look, cover, write, check' technique.

Spelling stage
Transitional with variations, semi-phonetic, phonetic and correct.

Number of players
Two or more.

What you need
Card to make base boards, 12 plain playing cards per child, one die.

How to make
Make one base board for each child, as shown, the numbers to correspond with those on the die. Make 12 word cards per child to fit on to the board using the children's personal spelling lists. They can be of any level and using any letter-string.

because	urgent	catch	when	different	weather
1	2	3	4	5	6
Know	their	timely	bean	dining	running

How to play

The object is to be the first to spell correctly 12 given words.

Give each child a base board, and place the spelling cards on the spaces face up.

The players take it in turns to roll a die. If the die lands on three, the player may choose to spell either word against three. The card is then turned face down.

The player then writes the word on a piece of rough paper. Their partner checks it – if it is correct, the card is removed from the board.

Play continues until one player has removed all the cards.

Note: If the die is rolled and both cards have already been removed, the player misses that go.

Silent bingo

Spelling aims

To encourage the 'look, cover, write, check' approach, to provide practice of letter-strings within words and to encourage careful observation of letter patterns.

Spelling stage

Transitional; with variations, phonetic and correct.

Number of players

Two to eight. It is possible to play this game with half classes or even whole classes, so long as each child has clear access to the words displayed.

What you need

Copy of sheet on page 88 for each player, 20 cards.

How to make

Make a set of 20 cards with print large enough for the whole group to see. Divide the cards into four sets, each set having five words with a common letter-string. On the reverse of each card, reproduce the symbol from the side of the sheet.

For example, letter-string -ing. Make cards for the following five words: king, string, thing, wing, sing. On the reverse you might choose to place a circle.

How to play

The object is to be the first to fill the card with the correct spelling of the displayed words.

Each child colours in a random choice of six squares, then all players place their pencils on the table or the floor.

The teacher displays the reverse side of the card, showing the symbol, and the players identify the line corresponding to that symbol. The teacher then displays the word for as long as he thinks advisable. No child may write at this point.

The teacher replaces the card, face down on the table, then the players pick up their pencils and write the word into any square on the correct line of their bingo sheet.

The teacher repeats this with other randomly chosen cards until a player completes her card and shouts 'Bingo!' The player's card is then checked by:
• pupils reading the words and then saying the letter names back to the teacher;

• the pupil identifying the letter-string for each symbol.

If she is correct, she is the winner and a new game can commence.

As an extension, ask each player to write a 'silly' sentence on the back of the bingo sheet, using the words from one line of the sheet. This is very popular and will cause much amusement.

Note: Some children may be inclined to copy the same square selection as their neighbour. If this happens, teachers could 'dot' the squares for each player to colour in before handing them to the group.

Variations

This is easily one of the most popular games for pupils at any developmental stage, from phonetic onwards:
• It can be played for medial vowels in three-letter words: eg cap, hat, mat, pan, tap. In this case, instead of putting symbols on the reverse of the cards and down the sides of the sheets, it is more valuable to give vowels.

• It can be played for any level of letter-strings. It is more effective when children begin to say letter names to themselves, generally requiring four or more letters to each word.

Spellasaurus

Spelling aim
To encourage word building through initial letters, blends and digraphs.

Spelling stage
Phonetic.

Number of players
One; or two or more.

What you need
Photocopy of dinosaur base on page 89 (one for each player), 12 horny backbone shapes made from card.

How to make
Write a word ending on the left-hand side of each card shape, and an initial letter, blend or digraph on the right-hand side: eg

How to play
The object is to place correctly spelt spines from the tail to the head of the dinosaur.

   Game for one player — spread the spines face up on the table. Let the child select spines which make words to enable him to go from the tail to the head.

Note: This is useful practice for the diffident reader and speller before they play in competition with a partner.

39

Game for two or more players – each player will need a dinosaur shape. Spread the spines face down on the table. Each player takes it in turns to pick up a spine from the table, which they may place on the dinosaur, starting at the tip of the tail. If the spine does not fit, the player returns it face down on the table and the next player has his turn. The winner is the first to complete his dinosaur and reach the head with correctly spelt combinations.

Note: It is possible to provide a checklist of acceptable words which the players can check against when they are uncertain.

Spelling dominoes

Spelling aims
To encourage children to look carefully at simple three-letter words and to match word to word.

Spelling stage
Transitional; with variations, phonetic and correct.

Number of players
Two to four. If children are at the beginning of their school life, it is better to have two players, or two plus an adult. If the children are slow at matching the words, four players means they have to wait too long between games.

What you need
Pieces of card (approx 9cm × 5cm).

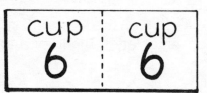

How to make
The teacher chooses simple words and writes them on the cards, as follows:

6 × 6 domino = cup × cup
6 × 5 domino = cup × hat
6 × 4 domino = cup × mat
6 × 3 domino = cup × pet
6 × 2 domino = cup × pin
6 × 1 domino = cup × hot
6 × 0 domino = cup × –
Therefore, the 5 × 5 domino = hat × hat, etc.

A card has to be made for each number combination, including zero. Use letter-strings as well as words.

How to play

The object is to get rid of all the dominoes from your hand. (It is helpful to discuss and show the letter-strings and words to be used before starting the game.)

Shuffle the cards. This can be done by the pupils 'stirring' the cards which have been spread out face down on the table.

Each player draws seven cards and may arrange them face up in front of him. The first player to find a double of any word places it face up on the table.

Players then take it in turns to match words to the dominoes displayed on the table. When a player is unable to put down a domino, he picks one up from the remaining cards and waits for his next turn.

The winner is the first player to get rid of all his dominoes.

Note: The players may find it necessary to walk around the table as the cards appear in different spatial orientation.

Variations

● The same game could be played using picture dominoes for very early matching.

● Three- and four-letter dominoes can be used for more developed players, with suggested emphasis on blends, digraphs or medial vowels.

● The game can be played by one child purely as a patience game, the object being to put down all the dominoes.

● As a final consolidation, a shared pad of paper could be passed around the players. Player 1 remembers a word from the game and says it to player 2, who then has to write the word. Player 1 checks to see if it is correct, If it is wrong, player 2 is asked to try again after being shown the word from the domino: ie look, cover, write and check. This continues round the players.

6 = ing
5 = and
4 = one
3 = aid
2 = as
1 = ate

Example shows the relationship between 'number' dominoes and 'letter-string' dominoes. NB Don't put numbers on when making the game.

										wing 6	thing 6
								hand 5	stand 5	and 5	King 6
						alone 4	done 4	one 4	sand 5	gone 4	ring 6
					maiden 3	paid 3	afraid 3	none 4	Said 3	island 5	aid 3	sing 6
			wash 2	gas 2	ask 2	raid 3	was 2	money 4	has 2	wand 5	as 2	bring 6
	separate 1	water 1	gate 1	hasn't 2	plate 1	laid 3	late 1	lonely 4	date 1	handle 5	ate 1	going 6
		pirate 1		case 2		maid 3		telephone 4		thousand 5		jingle 6

41

Split

Spelling aim
To encourage recognition and understanding of syllabification.

Spelling stage
Correct.

Number of players
Two to four. It is more difficult when more players are involved.

What you need
Large piece of paper, 15 cards, photocopy page 92.

How to make
Choose at least 15 words with two or more syllables (see page 92). They could be the months of the year, the days of the week, topic words, adjectives, and so on.

Make a list of the chosen words in print script, written large enough for the players to read them easily. Write each word on separate strips of card and then cut the card according to the syllable breaks: eg but/ter/fly.

How to play
Look at the word list and discuss syllabifications with the children. Can they recognise the beats within the word? Guide them to notice the presence of a vowel in each syllable and, if necessary, draw lines between each syllable.

Leave the list on display. The players may refer to it when they are uncertain and it encourages them to look closely at the words.

Each player takes seven cards from the central pile, and play begins by the first player picking up an extra card and deciding whether this helps to build any word using the cards in his hand.

If a player has a complete word, he may lay it down on the table. He then discards one card from his hand and places it face up next to the central pile. The next player may choose either to pick up from the discard pile or from the pack. He then tries to make a complete word, finally discarding one card from his hand.

When the central pile has been exhausted, the discard pile is turned over and becomes the new central pile.

Play continues until one player has used up all the cards in his hand to make complete words. Ten points may be awarded for each complete word exposed on the table. The winner is the first player to reach 50 points.
Note: Some players prefer to lay out all their cards in front of them.

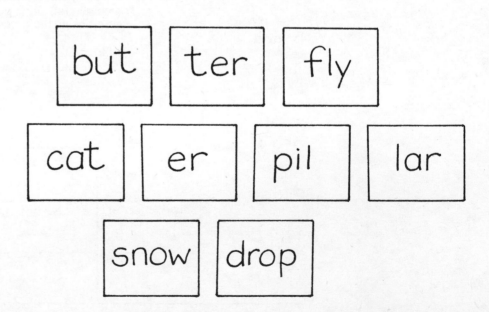

Spot the ladybird

Spelling aim
To encourage players to learn letter names and letter sounds.

Spelling stage
Semi-phonetic; with variation, phonetic.

Number of players
Two or three.

What you need
One copy of the ladybird on page 90 for each player, eight tiddly-winks for each player, 26 plain playing-cards.

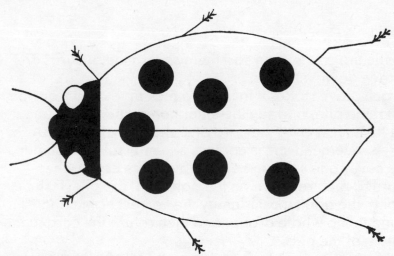

How to make
A complete set of alphabet cards is needed for this. Write the letter in upper and lower case on one side, and pick a picture card which starts with the letter sound on the reverse (see pages 111 onwards).

How to play
Shuffle the cards, then sort them so that the pictures are all face down in a pile.

Each player takes it in turns to pick up a card from the top of the pile, and say the letter name and letter sound. She then turns over the card and checks with the picture on the reverse. If she is correct, she may take a counter and cover one spot on her ladybird. The card is then returned picture down on the bottom of the pile. If she is wrong, the adult must identify the correct name and sound to the whole group, and then return the card to the bottom of the pile.

Play continues until one player has filled all the spots on her ladybird.

Note: This game is often played with young children, so it is advisable to have a figure of authority leading the game and helping the children with letters they identify incorrectly.

Take one, make one

Spelling aim
To encourage the recognition of rhyming words.

Spelling stage
Correct; with variations, transitional.

What you need
48 plain playing cards, copy page 93.

How to make
Write rhyming words on the cards in sets of four: ie 12 sets of four rhyming words (see list on page 93). Write the words large in the centre of the card and small in the top left-hand corner.

Mark the top of each card by a notch or line across the reverse side near the top. Homonyms may need illustration to aid understanding.

How to play
The object is to collect as many rhyming pairs as possible.

Shuffle the cards and deal them out equally between the players, who then sort the cards into pairs as far as possible.

Each player takes it in turns to put down on the table any pair held in his hand; only one pair is put down per turn.

The first player then holds out the cards in his hand (keeping the words hidden) for the player on his left to choose one card. This player looks to see if she has now got a matching pair or a pair previously not laid down. If so, she may place it on the table. She then turns to the player on her left and holds out her cards for the next player to choose, again not displaying the words.

The game continues until one player has no cards remaining in his hand.

Players score ten points for going out first, and ten points per pair of cards displayed on the table. They lose two points for every card still held in each hand. The player with the highest score wins.

Variations
● For very young children it is possible to do this with rhyming pictures rather than words.
● This need not be a rhyming game. It is equally possible to play it with pairs of letter-strings for any level.

Think and link

Spelling aim
To help children to recognise that words containing similar letter-strings do not necessarily sound the same.

Spelling stage
Correct.

Number of players
Three or more.

What you need
1 call sheet, photocopy grid on page 95 for each child.

How to make
Write several letter-strings that have previously been used and learned on to the board or a large sheet of paper.

How to play
Discuss with the children which five-letter-strings they feel most confident about recognising and using, then give each child a grid and ask them to write four of the nominated letter-strings five times over and one of the letter-strings four times over. These letter-strings are to be written in the top left-hand corner of each square (see diagram).

are	are	are	are	are
one	one	one	one	one
atch	atch	■	atch	atch
ead	ead	ead	ead	ead
rub	rub	rub	rub	rub

Note: Some children lose count of how many strings they have written. It is helpful if they use different colours to write or underline each string.

Discuss the tactical use of the shaded area in the centre of the grid, and how it might effect where they place which letter-string.

Call out the words from the call sheet (see page 94). The children write down the complete word in the centre of the square containing the appropriate letter-string. You will need to tick the words you have called, for reference when checking.

Players score two points for completing the first row, and then one point for each completed row across, down or diagonally. Check each completed row. The winner is the child with most points, the maximum score being 13.

46

Three in a bed

Spelling aim
To enhance recognition of letter-strings within words.

Spelling stage
Transitional; with variations, phonetic and correct.

Number of players
Two to six.

What you need
Plain playing cards.

How to make
For two players, make 24 cards — six cards for each letter-string. For four to six players, make 48 cards — two sets of the 24 cards.

Write the word in the centre of each card and in the top left-hand corner: eg chosen letter-string ui — penguin, suit, juice, suite, fruit, bruise. Mark the top back of each card or notch the top (see diagram).

How to play

The object is to get rid of all the cards from your hand by laying them down on the table.

Shuffle the cards by spreading them face down on the table and 'stirring' them.

Put all the cards with tops together, and deal out seven of these cards to each player. Place the remaining cards in a pile in the centre of the table. The first card is turned over face uppermost beside the pile.

The players look at their hands and sort them into groups. If a player has three of a kind, he may place them on the table when it is his turn. Players take it in turns to discard an unwanted card and to replace it from the pile or the top card of those discarded by previous players.

Players may go out by:
- laying down groups of three,
- adding any card to any run already on the table.

Players score ten points for going out and ten points for any set of three laid down on the table. They lose one point for every card still held in their hand.

Note: For the beginning reader and writer, three-letter words are adequate; four letters may cause confusion.

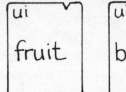 

Variations
- Collect three identical words.
- Collect three initial letter cards.
- Collect three final letter cards.
- Collect three medial vowel cards.
- Collect alphabet runs – any three consecutive letters would form a set. Older children would enjoy this, as it appears more challenging.

Traffic lights

Spelling aim
To encourage children to build words and deduce spelling.

Spelling stage
Correct.

Number of players
Two to six.

What you need
Pencils, coloured crayons, paper.

How to play
The object is to be the first to discover the hidden word.

The caller decides on a word and tells the group how many letters it contains. If it contains four letters, the first player suggests any four-letter word he can think of.

The caller then works out if any letters are the same. If the same letter occurs in the correct position, the caller says 'one circle green'. If the same letter occurs in an incorrect place, the caller says 'one circle red'.

The second player then offers a word with some of the same letters as the previous player. His word is similarly diagnosed.

As letters become eliminated, they are crossed off the alphabet. The game continues until the word is guessed. eg The secret word is 'what'.
The players are told 'four letters'.
The first player suggests 'come' = no colours.
The second player suggests 'take' = two red circles.
The third player suggests 'hunt' = one green circle.

The fourth player suggests 'want' = two green, one red.
The fifth player suggests 'what' = correct.

This game is really for competent, confident spellers. In order to make it simpler, the caller could identify the letter and players would ring this on the left-hand side: eg The secret word is 'what'.

The first player suggests 'come' = no letters.
The second player suggests 'take' = caller agrees 'a' in word but not correct place, etc.

The game continues along these lines until the word is identified.

What is it?

Spelling aim
To enable children to identify letter shapes and names.

Spelling stage
Semi-phonetic.

Number of players
Two to eight.

How to play
Sit the children in a line, one behind the other.

Trace a simple letter shape on the first child's back with your finger, and ask her to trace this shape on to the next player's back. This continues until the last player has the letter drawn on his back. He is then asked if he knows what letter has been traced.

The play recommences with a different first player.
Note: Discuss with the children the letter name and shape.

Variations
• Play as above in two teams of four. The team whose last player can identify the letter gets a point. The winning team is the first one to reach four points.
• For more advanced children, again in teams, the first player has an upper case letter traced on her back. She then has to trace a matching lower case letter on the next team member's back. This player has to reinterpret the letter into upper case. The winning team is the one whose last player correctly identifies the original letter.
• These activities could be used in movement lessons. Here the children could 'walk' letters and others identify the letter by name.
Note: All the activities lend themselves to discussing the starting and finishing points of letters.

Word clock patience

Spelling aims
To encourage players to make simple two-, three- or four-letter words and to become familiar with word building.

Spelling stage
Phonetic; with variations, transitional.

Number of players
One.

What you need
52 plain playing cards.

How to make
Make letter cards as follows:
consonants z, x, v, q, j = one card;
all remaining consonants = two cards;
all vowels a, e, i, o, u = three cards.
   Laminate the cards if possible, or they will get very worn.

How to play
The aim is to use all the cards up in words. (This is very difficult.)
   Arrange the first 12 cards from the pile in a circle face up, representing the numbers on a clock. Put the 13th card in the centre of the circle.
   The player may pick up cards from anywhere in the circle to make a simple word. The spaces left are filled by cards from the pack, and the player then endeavours to make new words.

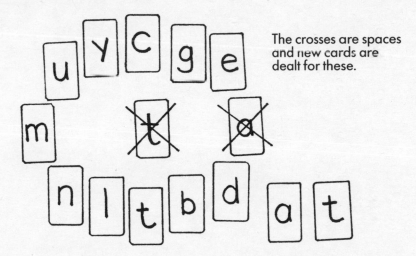

The crosses are spaces and new cards are dealt for these.

The player must use cards in the clock face to start the word: ie the letter 'a' given above cannot be in the middle of a word.
   Players could start with 30 points and lose one point for every card unused.

Variations
• The letters of the clock face could be used in the final letter position or middle letter position.
• The number of letters could be restricted: ie only three-letter words or only four-letter words.

Spelling activities

Whole class activities

Around the world

What you need
No special requirements.

What to do
Collecting words from various places around the world can be an interesting ongoing activity. It may be possible to have an outline map on the wall and to link the word to the country of origin.

Children could collect and discuss the words and see how many they can find within each half-term. Here are some examples:

Word	Country	Meaning
bungalow	India	balcony
port	France	door
graffiti	Italy	writing
blitz	Germany	lightening
discotheque	France	record-playing
cinema	Greece	motion

Follow-up
Extend this search for words to include other languages and scripts. For example: hito = man, l'homme = man.

Creation

What you need
Pencils, paper.

What to do
Give the children a word of some length and see how many words they can make, using only the letters given. Writing the words within an outline shape gives the activity more appeal. For example:

Formabet

Group size
Divide the class into two teams.

What you need
Pencils, paper.

a ant   h hen
b bear   i iguana
c cat   J Jellyfish
d dog   k kangaroo
e elephant L lion
f fish   m monkey
g goat   n newt

What to do
The teacher asks the children to write down a word on a given topic. The child then passes this to the next player who adds a word on the same topic, maintaining alphabetical order.

The aim is to see which team can produce the first alphabet of words.

Suggested topics: town alphabet, four-letter word alphabet, animal alphabet.

Depending on the 'age' of the class it is possible to award marks for unusual words. In this game the teacher decides the duration of the game. The teams could work together to suggest words. When the time is up, one team leader reads out her list. If another team has an identical word they score only one mark each. If a team has a unique word they score two marks. The winner is the team with the most marks.

Ladders and stairs

What you need
No special requirements.

What to do
The teacher puts up a strip of paper with a word written at the bottom (the most common are four- and three-letter words). The children take turns to change one letter at a time to create a new word. For example:

mean		saw
meat		sad
meet		bad
feet		bed
feel		bet
peel		bit

Variation
A variation on this is to build a stairway of words or a sentence where children take it in turns to use the last letter of the previous word as the first letter of the next word:

duck
in
goat
im
eggs
a
duck

52

Multiplication

What you need
No special requirements.

What to do
The first child writes a noun at the top right-hand corner of the board. The children take it in turns to add a word to describe it until no more can be thought of.

This game can be played in teams where the teacher gives the first word and the teams have to expand it:

```
eg                      tree
                  apple tree
             old apple tree
       gnarled old apple tree
```

Later in the day the children could be asked to write down the longest phrase that they can remember.

Think again

What you need
No special requirements.

What to do
Most children enjoy writing on the blackboard, so let each child have a turn at writing a word on the board. His word should be the first one he thinks of when he sees the previous word:
eg Teacher writes 'ball'.
First child writes 'racquet'.
Second child writes 'tennis'.
Third child writes 'summer'.

Each child should explain the association to the rest of the class.

Think of another

Group size
Whole class.

What you need
No special requirements.

What to do
Encourage the children to use more interesting words instead of the most common. For example:

he said	she walked	nice	big
whispered	crawled	gorgeous	gross
shouted	sidled	pleasant	immense
argued	jumped	pretty	huge

   This collection could be displayed on the wall and used in writing periods, and the children could add to the list.

Variation
As a variation, the teacher could write a list of common phrases and the children have to think of one word to replace them. This could become a kind of beat-the-teacher activity, where the class has to try to fill in all the words before the end of the day. This might also encourage the use of a thesaurus.

very small	– tiny
very lazy	– sluggard
lost in thought	– preoccupied
a small amount of money	– pittance
to clear from blame	– exonerate
a hundred years	– century

Tongue-twisters

What you need
Pencils, paper.

What to do
A class competition to write the most amusing or difficult tongue-twister is great fun. The children can choose any letter to be the initial and endeavour to make up a sentence using words beginning with that letter:
eg Traditional tongue-twisters:
Peter Piper picked a peck of pickled pepper.
or Auntie Annie ambles amiably along an awfully ancient alleyway.
   This is a useful way to draw attention to an initial letter sound or blend.

Twenty questions

What you need
No special requirements.

What to do
This is always a popular game, especially with the older children. The teacher or a child thinks of a word (preferably associated with a topic or project being undertaken). The class may ask up to 20 questions to try to discover what the word is. The person who correctly identifies it and spells it on the board becomes the new word thinker.

The word of the day

What you need
Card.

What to do
The teacher chooses a word and writes it up on the board or makes a card which is pinned up in the same place each day. This is left for some time so that all the children have sufficient time to notice it. At a chosen time, the teacher takes down the word and, later, asks the class to write it down.

As the children become used to this activity, several variations might enliven it. The teacher could choose to display it in numerous different locations, so that the children have to look carefully at classroom notices etc, to identify the word.

Each class member must endeavour to use the word in a conversation with the teacher. If she achieves this, then some recognition could be given. This is a challenging activity and helps the child to make the word part of her learned vocabulary.

The teacher could ask the class to see how many words they can find within the letter order of the word: eg brother – broth, other, rot, her, he.

Group activities

The hot seat game

Group size
Six.

What you need
A sheet of paper for each child.

What to do
One child is selected from the group and stands by the teacher's desk until the others are ready. Each member of the group chooses a word that he can spell to challenge with, and writes it on his paper. Each player starts with three lives.

The child returns to the group and each member takes it in turns to challenge her with his word. She writes this boldly on her sheet of paper and then checks with the challenger. If she spells the word correctly, she collects five points; if she makes a mistake, she loses a life.

After each member has challenged her, or when she has lost all three lives, her marks are totalled and the next child is selected for the hot seat. A dictionary may only be used in cases of dispute.

The teacher should be careful to choose groups of roughly the same spelling stage. Using words that have been in recent topics or perhaps chosen from 'word of the day' (see page 55), can reinforce useful spellings.

The word mobile

Group size
Groups of four children or divide the class into groups.

What you need
Pencils, paper.

What to do
Divide the class into groups and ask each group to make a mobile of words: eg words for the topic, words about colours, phrases, sentences, a story, a poem, questions using 'who', 'what', 'where', 'when' and 'why'.

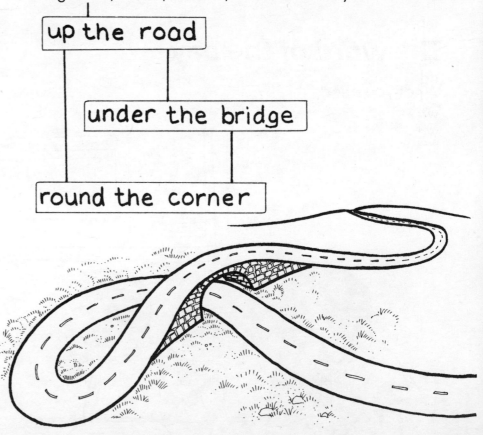

Activities for two

Abracadabra

What you need
Pencils, paper.

What to do
The first player thinks of a word and writes down the first letter on a sheet of paper. The second player thinks of a word beginning with the letter given, and adds the second letter. The first player uses these two letters and adds a third, and so on.

Either player may challenge the word. If the player who wrote the last letter cannot produce a correctly spelt word, the challenger gets a point; if he can prove his word, he gets a point. The player who finishes a word loses a point. For example:
t, te, tel, tele = challenge
Second player claims 'television' and wins a point.

Variation
The first player thinks of a word and substitutes dashes for each letter. She then gives one letter from the word in the correct place: _ _ _ _ _ r. Her opponent may guess the whole word or ask for another letter. The first player offers _ _ _ c _ r (the word is 'soccer'). This continues until the word is guessed correctly. For every gap not filled, the guesser wins two points, and for every letter given the chooser wins two points. The first player to reach 20 points is the winner.

Criss-cross

What you need
Pencils, photocopy grid on page 96 for each player.

What to do
Each player has a copy of the crossword grid on page 96.

The players take it in turns to choose a word they can spell. The minimum number of letters in a word should be agreed beforehand.

The first player says his word, then both players write it anywhere they like on their own grid. The second player nominates a word and this is also written on the grid. This continues until both players are unable to add any more words to the crossword.

Words may be written horizontally, vertically or diagonally. If any player is uncertain how to spell the word, the caller must write it down in print script for him. If a word will not fit, the player misses his go, but he may offer one for his grid next time.

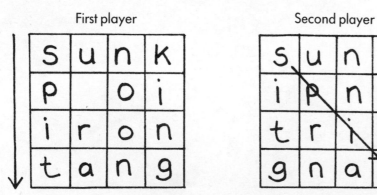

First player   Second player

First word offered was 'spit'.

58

Hangman

What you need
Pencil, paper.

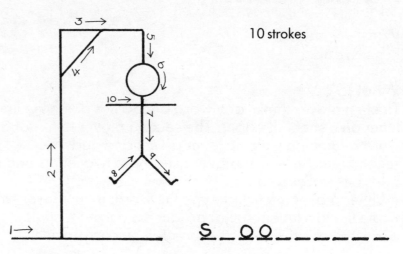

10 strokes

S _ O O _ _ _ _ _ _ _

incorrect letters : TARH

What to do
One child thinks of a word and writes clear dashes for each letter. Their opponent suggests a possible letter and, if it is in the chosen word, it is written on the dash in the correct space. If it is wrong, the first player begins to draw the picture below, and records the incorrect letter.

If the word is guessed before the picture is complete, the opponent wins, but if the picture is completed before the word is guessed, the 'hangman' wins.

Letter-string race

What you need
Card, paper, pencils.

What to do
The teacher gives each player a card with a letter string
of similar difficulty written on it. The first player to write
ten words containing the letter string is the winner.
Note: It is possible to play this in groups, but it is much
easier to manage in pairs.

eg | ind | oat
| blind | boat
| find | coat
| wind | float

Activities for individuals

Back-to-front

What you need
Pencil, paper

What to do
To encourage the children to experiment with words, the
teacher or child chooses a word and writes it down the
left-hand side of the page. Then, leaving sufficient space
between the two sides, she writes it backwards up the
right-hand side.

The child then fills in the space between the vertical
words, starting with a letter on the left and ending with a
letter on the right. For example:

```
B A T C H
ELECTRIC
A       A
C       E
H       B
```

Variation

A variation on this is to use acrostic poems. The teacher or child writes any noun down the left-hand side of the sheet and the child tries to think of words, beginning with each letter, which describe the words. For example: mountain

Mighty
Old
Unattainable
Noble
Tall
Ancient
Important
Noiseless

Codes

What you need
Pencil, paper.

What to do
Cracking codes is another popular activity which ensures that children pay careful attention to words and their structure. They can be created in various ways, but many substitute different letters, numbers or symbols for the letters of the message. For example:

	A	B	C	D	E	F	G
number	1	2	3	4	5	6	7
letter	Z	Y	X	W	V	U	T
symbol	O	–	△	□	⊘	÷	+

Letter-shape words

What you need
Pencil, paper.

What to do
Large letter-shapes – drawn by either the teacher or the child, can be filled with words starting or ending with the letter:

Letter-string patterns

What you need
Pencil, paper.

What to do
These patterns help hand/eye co-ordination for common letter-strings. As far as possible they should be written in a continuous cursive handwriting style. Children quickly get used to writing 'th' together, so when they have to write the word 'thought', if they break their handwriting after the 'g', they are likely to reverse the 'ht' to 'th'.

   These shapes can be anything the child wishes to do eg

Newspaper search

What you need
Newspapers.

What to do
Get the child to find any published printed paper and then see how quickly he can find a chosen letter pattern and identify it using a highlighter pen. Children enjoy doing this by timing themselves against an egg-timer.
    They could be asked to find:
- one letter: eg 't'
- one-letter words: eg 'I'
- two letters: eg 'er'
- two-letter words
- letter-strings: eg 'out', 'str', 'ield' etc.
This can be made more exciting if a definite target is given for the child to find.

Shape poetry or calligrams

What you need
Pencils, paper.

What to do
Shape poetry can be written with one word or many words attached to the subject. The idea is to get the words to form a picture of the subject eg 'The sea'

WAVES WAVES WAVES WAVES WAVES
breaking   breaking   breaking   breaking
sand   sand   sand   ROCKS   sand

    Calligrams are words written is such a way as to reflect their own meaning.

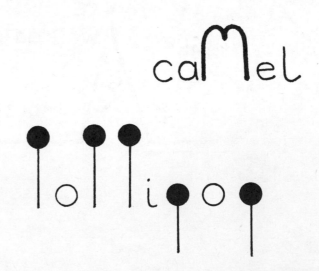

Silly sentences

What you need
Pencil, paper.

What to do
Getting the children to write sentences with certain restrictions can be a challenge and also enables them to concentrate on the words.

1 Take any word and ask the child to write a sentence using each letter in turn:

eg headmaster

He enrolled a dog more appropriately since the elephants revolted.

2 Or ask them to create a sentence without using a chosen letter:

eg No 'e'

The dog was missing for four days.

The <u>queen</u> fell over in the <u>quarry</u>.

3 They could try to fill a gap in a given sentence in as many ways as possible:

eg The _____ fell over in the _____.

The child writes as many different sentences as possible.

4 As a variation, give the child a list of letters that they must use to start each word in the gaps:

eg 'qu'

The queen fell over in the quarry.

The teacher writes a sentence, omitting chosen letters:

eg The vowels

C–N Y— P–T –LL TH– V–W–LS –NT– TH–S– SP–C–S?

Word search

What you need
Copy page 96.

What to do
The teacher writes words which she wants the children to learn, or which are specific to a chosen topic, on to a squared grid (photocopy master on page 96). When the words have been written, fill in the blank squares with random letters. Then ask the children to try to find the words and list them.

Explain that the words can be found vertically, horizontally, diagonally, backwards and bottom-up:

eg Topic: road safety

Y	S	L	O	W	K	L	A	W	R
A	T	R	A	F	F	I	C	U	G
L	O	O	K	Q	O	G	N	R	R
E	P	A	T	H	R	H	R	I	E
R	E	D	W	A	I	T	U	D	E
T	X	S	C	L	I	S	T	E	N

Children may like to make word searches for each other.

63

Using a dictionary

A dictionary is 'a book dealing with the words of a language so as to set forth their orthography, pronunciation, signification and use, their synonyms, derivation and history, or at least some of these; the words are arranged in some stated order, now usually alphabetical; a word-book, vocabulary, lexicon.'

Shorter Oxford English Dictionary (1983)

Although dictionaries are a principal resource for competent spellers, they can be confusing and unhelpful for individuals who have not attained this level.

The definition given above gives some indication of the range and complexity of a dictionary. Children are constantly told to use a dictionary to help with spelling, yet an adult more frequently uses one to establish the meaning of a word.

Using a dictionary requires conscious teaching, and should be included as part of a spelling and language development programme.

Children need to be able to do the following:
• Know their alphabet order – when this is secure, they should be able to open the dictionary at or near the letter they require.
• Know and understand the four major divisions: ie A–D, E–L, M–R, S–Z. This can be helped by mnemonics

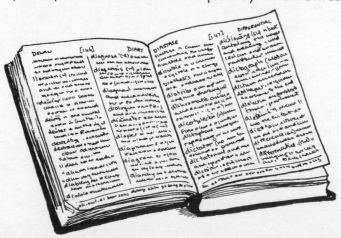

along the lines of   A-untie E-dna M-akes S-weets; A-my E-el M-oves S-ilently.
• Understand that words are organised according to the alphabetical order of all their letters, not just the first.
• Understand that words are listed under the root word. Children may not realise that they will not always be able to find such words as 'advising' or 'excessively'.
• Understand that most words are listed in the singular – plurals often cause concern: eg 'mice' is not listed in the substantial *Oxford Illustrated Dictionary* (985 pages).
• Understand the reason for the guide words at the top of the pages.
• Know how to read a dictionary – a broken stilted read is required; inexperienced children may try to read it as though it is a story book.

Spelling dictionaries

There are several dictionaries whose main aim is to aid spelling. They do not provide definitions, so that it is far quicker to find the word the child wants to spell.

'If I can't spell a word, how can I find it?' it a frequent and valid complaint. Pupils have to be taught to explore possible alternatives: for instance, they must try both 'f' and 'ph' for that similar initial letter sound.

Some spelling dictionaries offer the user the common or possible alternatives. These dictionaries should be included in a classroom dictionary selection and should not be condemned. They have been found especially useful to many children entering secondary school.

A teacher's aim should be to encourage children to refer readily to a dictionary. It may be that they start to use a dictionary for spelling, but if they also realise that it is a source of fascinating information about words, then not only are they on the way to becoming good spellers, but they may also develop a life-long interest in language.

Activities for promoting dictionary skills

For the following activities, the children will need to be able to refer to the alphabet, either on a strip on the table or at eye-level on the classroom wall. They need to be able to identify each letter by its name (see alphabet games on pages 19–20).

The whole alphabet is frequently too long to learn in one chunk. It is better to break it into manageable sections: ie the four quarters.

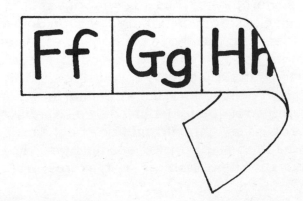

Attack-a-track

Group size
Individuals.

What you need
Photocopy pages 97 and 98 for each child.

What to do
Get the child to track the alphabet in its correct order from the nonsense words given on pages 97 and 98. Explain that the child may not return to a letter: for example, having found 'd' in the fifth 'word', she may not find 'e' in the fourth 'word'.

This kind of activity is easy to make, enjoyable for the children, and can even be prepared by one child for another. Children should be able to complete the activity in well under two minutes. They will enjoy timing themselves until they achieve this time.

Alphabet mazes

Group size
Individuals.

What you need
Photocopy pages 99 to 102 for each child.

What to do
Give the child photocopies of pages 99 to 102 and ask them to get to the centre of the maze in alphabetical order. Some children may be able to cope with this activity without reference to an alphabet strip.

Simply mask the letters and make your own maze as required.

Plastic letters

Group size
Individuals.

What you need
Plastic letters of the alphabet (available from most toy shops and stationers).

What to do
Plastic letters can be used to practise alphabet order and the alphabet quarters.

It is possible to make a set of cards instead, but if lower case letters are being used, do ensure that a writing line is provided to show the correct orientation of the letter.

The zigzag strip

Group size
Individuals.

What you need
Paper strips, pencils, crayons.

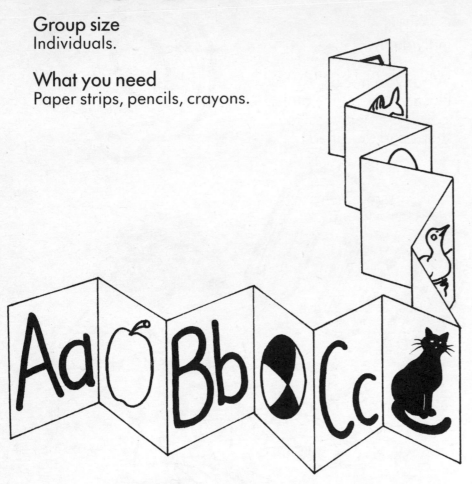

What to do
Get the children to make themselves an alphabet zigzag by folding a 7cm wide strip of paper into a zigzag so that the first crease is on the left, then putting upper and lower case letters on each sheet, opening the flap and drawing a picture starting with the initial sound on the other side.

Teaching the quarter divisions

Group size
Individuals.

What you need
A dictionary, card or string to use as markers.

What to do
Get the children to open the dictionary in the middle, and discuss why the letter 'M' is there. Ask them to divide the section A–M in the middle. Why does the letter 'E' now fall on the quarter? Now divide the section M–Z in half. Why does the letter 'S' mark the quarter?

If the children have their own dictionaries it is useful to either mark the top of the pages of the closed book to indicate the four sections, or to use a piece of string or card to divide each section.

This exercise helps to develop orthographic understanding: ie 'G' is not the start of the second quarter, since there are far more words beginning with A–E. Is this the same in a French or German dictionary?

Second-letter order

Group size
Individuals or small groups.

What you need
A dictionary for each child.

What to do
Once children have become familiar with their alphabetic order they can begin looking at second-letter order.

Get them to race against each other, or have team races, putting simple words into alphabetical order: eg cat, cow; goat, girl; net, nine; vein, van etc.

Ask them to find a word: eg 'mouse'. Will they go forwards or backwards to find 'mountain'?

Try to ensure that words are chosen from each quarter.

The ABC

'Twas midnight in the schoolroom
And every desk was shut,
When suddenly from the alphabet
Was heard a loud 'Tut-tut!'

Said A to B, 'I don't like C;
His manners are a lack,
For all I ever see of C
Is a semi-circular back!'

'I disagree', said D to B,
'I've never found C so.
From where I stand, he seems to be
An uncompleted O.'

C was vexed, 'I'm much perplexed,
You criticize my shape.
I'm made like that, to help spell Cat
and Cow and Cool and Cape.'

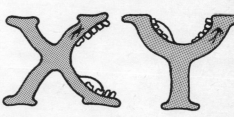

'He's right', said E; said F. 'Whoopee!'
Said G, ' 'Ip, 'ip, 'ooray!'
'You're dropping me', roared H to G.
'Don't do it please I pray!'

'Out of my way', L said to K.
'I'll make poor I look ILL.'
To stop this stunt, J stood in front.
And presto! ILL was JILL.

'U know', said V, 'that W
Is twice the age of me,
For as a Roman V is five
I'm half as young as he.'

X and Y yawned sleepily,
'Look at the time!' they said.
'Let's all get off to beddy byes.'
They did, then, 'Z,Z,Z.'

Spike Milligan

Tips for teachers

The basis of improving a child's spelling is to help them to learn to spell the words *they* want to use in free writing. This will necessarily be individual to each child. It appears a daunting task to the busy teacher to decide how to collect each child's spelling and then how to help each child on an individual basis. The following suggestions are ways in which the teacher might try to do this. Ask the pupil to draw a wide margin down the side of the page. Let the pupil write his narrative without fear of making spelling errors. When he wants a word that he feels he does not know how to spell he leaves a gap and then continues. The teacher writes the word in the margin for him. These words are the basis of his own list. Even more important are the words he thinks he can spell. These words must be learned correctly before they become too ingrained. They are the priority words for his personal list. The child then copies these words into his word book or writes them on to cards so that he can play such games as noughts and crosses, 'Escape' or 'Self check'.

The centralised word book

It is a good idea to have one substantial word book for the whole class, kept beside the teacher, and organised alphabetically. When a child wants a word, she first checks to see if she can find it in the class book, perhaps asking another child to help her to find her word.

If it is not in the word book, she asks the teacher to write it in. She then studies it for as long as necessary, returns to her place and writes the word. She may either then or later check this spelling, and return to look again as many times as she needs to, but she may not copy.

It is advisable for the teacher only to write in this book, so that letter-shape consistency and correct spellings are maintained — we hope!

The children's spelling books

Rather than organise the children's spelling books alphabetically, it is easier to chart the children's progress if the spellings they have chosen to learn are written clearly on to one page with the date at the top.

In this way, the teacher can check back to see if words are recurring week after week, as well as showing the child the improvement she is making throughout the year.

Say the name

Whatever stage of spelling development a child has reached, spellings should be written down and the alphabetic names said to the child.

This is also a point that parents need to know. 'How does it sound?' is not helpful to children trying to spell.

Those awkward words

Some words constantly give problems. As well as discussing the 'nasty bits' in the word, children enjoy making up their own mnemonics for the word.

One 11-year-old suddenly said 'I know how to remember "catch" – don't let the cat catch the mouse.'

Below are some of the more famous mnemonics which may help:

A piece of pie.

Never believe a lie.

'Necessary' has one collar and two socks.

A special agent is someone in the CIA.

'Difficulty' is often remembered from the spelling rhyme:

'Mrs D, Mrs I, Mrs FFI, Mrs C, Mrs U, Mrs I TY.'

A piece of pie

The magic carpet

Some children seem to have difficulty in managing to recall words using the 'look, cover, write, check' approach. If this occurs, try the 'magic carpet'.

Stick a piece of 'baize' fablon (10cm × standard width of roll – available from hardware stores for lining cutlery drawers) on to a sheet of card. When a pupil constantly makes the same spelling mistake, go through the following procedure:

- Write the word for the child on a piece of card.
- The child looks at the word, then says the letter names and finally the complete word: eg F, I, S, H, fish.
- The child then traces with the index finger of his writing hand the letters of the word on the magic carpet, again saying the letter names and finally the complete word.
- He repeats this as often as he wishes and then writes the word into his spelling book or on to spelling cards.
- This approach helps greatly to eradicate the common spelling errors.

Photocopiable material

Suggested blends for Blend and build (see page 21)

Two letter blends
bl, br, cl, cr, dr, fl, fr, gl, gr, pl, pr, sl, sm, sn, sp, st, sw, tr,
tw.
Three letter blends
scr, spl, spr, squ, str.
All possible blend endings for use with blend and build

a	e	i	o	u
ab	ell	ib	ob	ub
ack	em	ick	ock	ug
ad	ep	id	og	um
ag	esh	ig	om	ung
an	ess	ill	ong	ush
and		im	op	ust
ank		in	ost	
ang		ink	ot	
ant		ing		
am		int		
ap		ip		
art		ipt		
ash		isp		
at		ist		
		it		

Blend and build check list (see page 21)

bl = black, bland, blank, bless, blink, blob, block, blot, blush.

br = bran, brand, brag, brash, brat, brick, brim, bring, brush.

cl = clack, clad, clan, clang, clam, clap, clash, click, clink, cling, clip, clock, clog, clop, clot, club, clung.

cr = crab, crack, crag, crain, crank, crash, cress, crib, crick, crisp, crop, crust.

dr = drab, drag, dram, drank, drat, dress, drill, drink, drip, drop, drug.

fl = flab, flack, flag, flan, flap, flash, flat, flesh, flick, fling, flint, flip, flit, flog, flop, flung, flush.

fr = fresh, frill, frock, frog, from, frost.

gl = glad, gland, glib, glint, glum.

gr = grab, gram, gran, grand, grid, grill, grain, grin, grip, grit, grog, grub.

pl = plan, plank, plop, plot, plug, plum, plush.

pr = prank, pram, press, prick, prig, prim, print, prop.

sl = slab, slack, slag, slam, slang, slap, slash, slat, slid, slick, slim, slink, sling, slip, slit, slog, slop, slot, slub, slug, slum, slung, slush.

sn = snack, snag, snap, snich, snip, snob, snug, snub.

sp = spam, span, spank, spat, spell, spick, spill, spin, spit, spot.

st = stab, stack, stag, starch, stank, stash, stem, step, stick, still, string, stink, stint, stock, stop, stub, stung.

sw = swag, swam, swan, swat, swell, swig, swill, swim, swing, swot, swum, swung.

tr = track, tram, trash, trick, trill, trip, trim, trot, trug.

tw = twang, twig, twill, twin, twist, twit.

scr = scram, scrap, script, scrub, scrum.

spl = splash, splint, split.

spr = sprang, sprig, spring, sprint, sprung.

squ = squib, squid, squint.

str = strand, strap, stress, string, strip, strong.

Blend and build (see page 21)

Suggested words for Burglar Bill (see page 23)

Silent letters

b	d	gn	h		k	l	u	w
bomb	badge	gnash	heir		knack	calf	guard	wrap
comb	budge	gnat	honest		knit	half	guess	wreck
dumb	dodge	gnome	honour		knob	folk	guest	wren
limb	edge	reign	hour		knot	talk	guide	write
lamb	fudge	design	why		knelt	walk	guilt	who
numb	hedge	resign	what		knife	yolk	league	whole
tomb	judge	sign	when		kneel	stalk	buy	whom
crumb	ledge		whip		knew	chalk	guy	wrist
plumb	lodge		while		knight	calm	boulder	wrong
thumb	nudge		whine			palm	shoulder	
doubt	bridge		white					
	grudge		which			psalm	buoy	
	sledge		wheat					
	sludge		wheel					
	trudge		where					

List of possible words for The cup cap game (see page 25)

For beginners, three letters are sufficient:

cup cup cap
mop map mop
bat ban bat
hit hit hid
gas gas gap
bed bid bid

As soon as the players get used to the game it is more effective to move to four letters:

last last mast
skin skip skin
kind find find
gift lift gift
lady baby lady
belt felt belt

A further step would be to offer varying middle letters:

dinner   diner   dinner
chose   chose   choose
advice   advise   advise
potato   potatoes   potato
runny   running   runny
scrapping scraping   scrapping

Cup cap grid (see page 25)

6	5	4	3	2	1

Useful for Dragon snap (see page 26)

Back to front cards

tap	pat
pot	top
bad	dab
stab	bats
strap	parts
liar	rail
golf	flog
tug	gut
mug	gum
wolf	flow
snip	pins
evil	live
loop	pool
dog	god
stop	pots
trams	smart
raw	war
pans	snap
peek	keep
stun	nuts
sleep	peels
doom	mood
star	rats

Homonyms

weight	wait
check	cheque
meat	meet
boar	bore
rode	road
maid	made
roll	role
tale	tail
been	bean
hare	hair
peace	piece
blew	blue
sore	soar
bough	bow
write	right
flower	flour
sight	site
sail	sale
bear	bare
heal	heel
rain	reign
soul	sole
great	grate

Escape grid (see page 27)

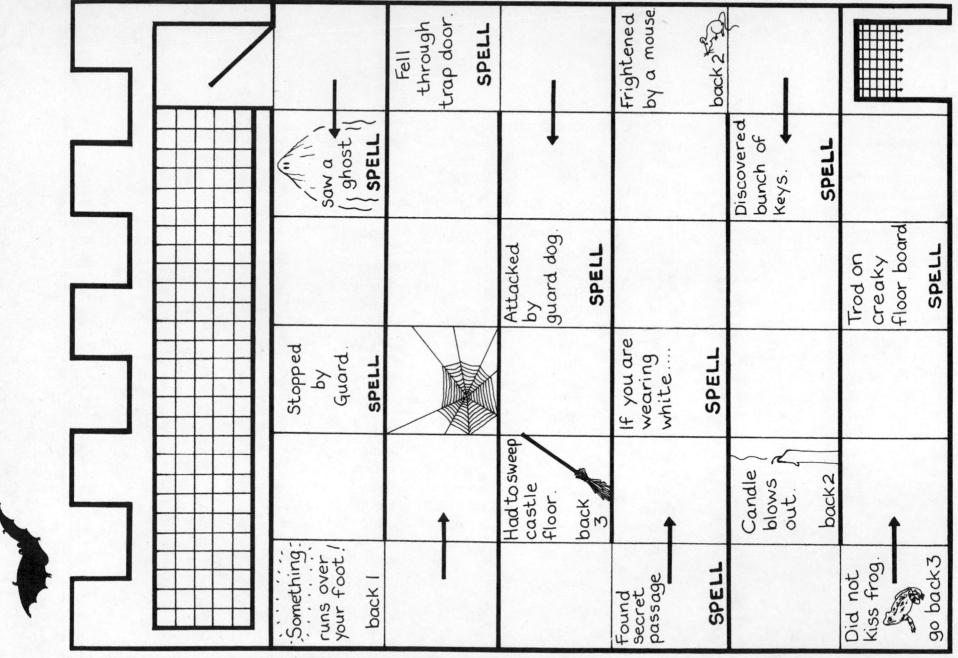

Fell through trap door. **SPELL**

Frightened by a mouse. back 2

Saw a ghost **SPELL**

Discovered bunch of keys. **SPELL**

Attacked by guard dog. **SPELL**

Trod on creaky floor board **SPELL**

Stopped by Guard. **SPELL**

If you are wearing white..... **SPELL**

Had to sweep castle floor. back 3

Candle blows out. back 2

Something runs over your foot! back 1

Found secret passage **SPELL**

Did not kiss frog. go back 3

Useful words for Hide and seek (see page 29)

List of words commonly misspelt

absence	embarrass	privilege
across	excellent	queue
address	excitement	quiet
all right	extremely	quite
amount		really
appearance	favourite	receive
argument	friend	restaurant
awkward	guarantee	rhyme
beautiful	guard	ridiculous
believe	immediately	seize
because	in between	separate
bicycle	in fact	sincerely
Britain	in front	successful
business	interested	surprise
college	library	
completely	loneliness	they
conscience	meant	tomorrow
definite	necessary	tries
description	no one	unnecessary
desperately	nuisance	until
develop	paid	vehicle
disappear	peculiar	weird

Words useful for Lucky dip (see page 33)

Compound words

afternoon	herself
anything	himself
afterwards	however
anyone	island
birthday	indoors
breakfast	itself
became	keyboard
blackberry	nightmare
bulldozer	overcome
carpet	postcard
cloakroom	railway
cupboard	rucksack
classroom	rainbow
donkey	shellfish
downstairs	snowman
everyone	tomorrow
eyesight	tonight
farewell	today
farmyard	underhand
goodbye	wallpaper
greyhound	woodworm

Omega trail (see page 34)

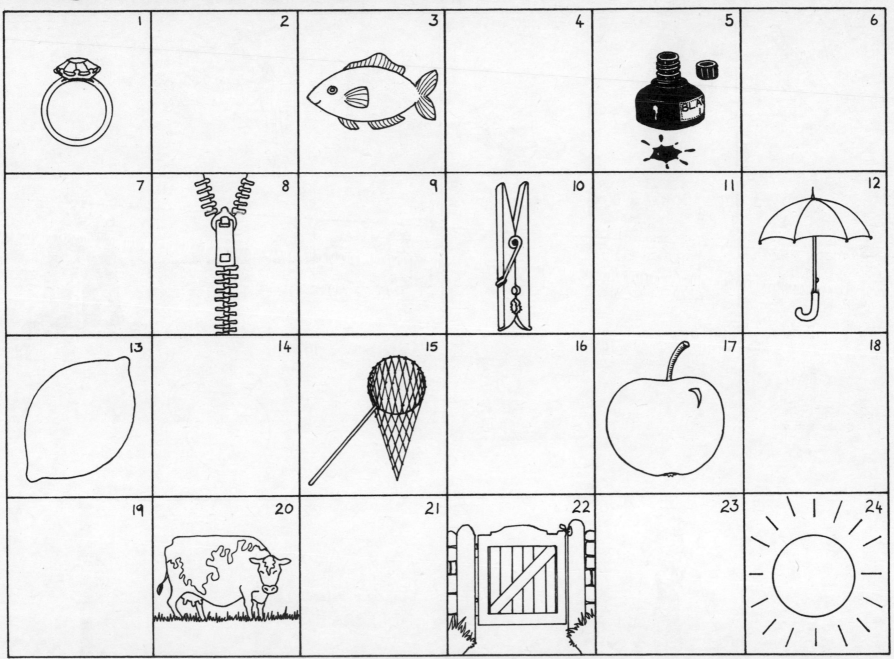

Omega trail (see page 34)

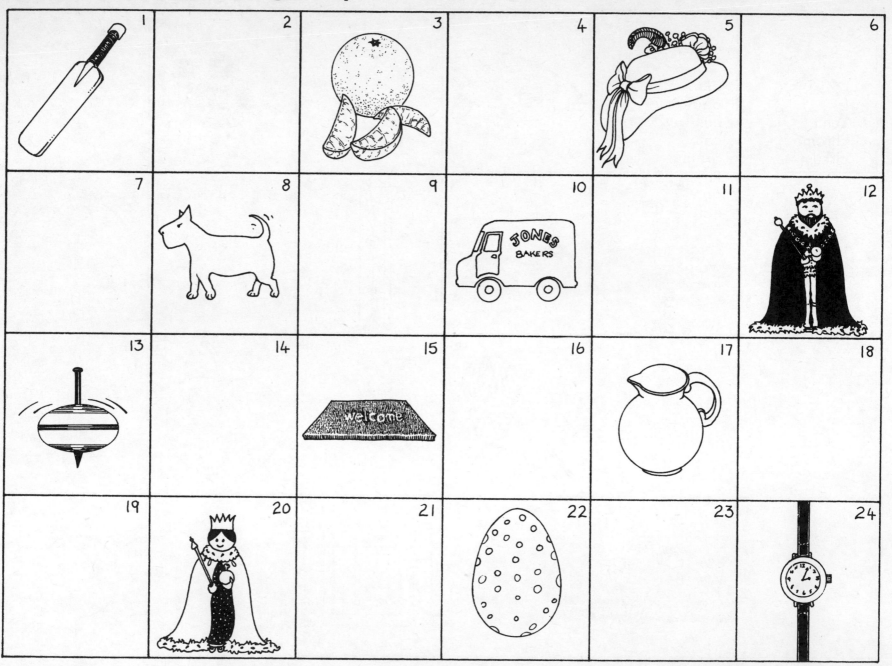

List of prefixes and meanings for Roots (see page 35)

a	without, none		a	without, none
ante	before		iso	equal
anti	against		mal	bad
centi	hundred		manu	hand
chromo	colour		mega	large
circum	around		micro	small
co	together		multi	many
contra	against		mono	one
demi	half		no	not
hemi	half		omni	all
homo	same		photo	light
hydro	water		pseudo	false
hyper	too much		retro	backwards
hypo	too little		sub	under
intra	within		super	above
inter	between		ultra	extreme

Silent bingo grid (see page 37)

⬤			
✚			
▲			
◼			

Spellasaurus (see page 39)

Spot the ladybird (see page 43)

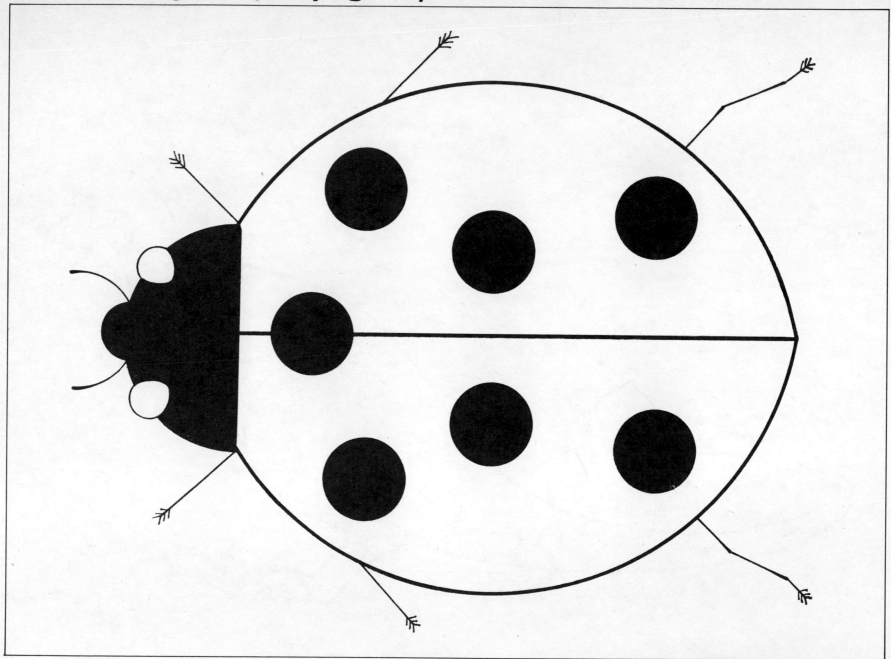

Words that can be used for Spelling dominoes (see page 40)

aid	as	ate	ing	and	one
afraid	as	ate	bring	abandon	alone
aid	ask	date	cling	and	bone
laid	disaster	gate	fling	hand	done
maid	flask	late	going	handle	gone
maiden	gas	pirate	jingle	island	lonely
paid	has	plate	king	sand	money
raid	hasn't	separate	ring	sandals	none
said	last	water	string	stand	one
	nasty		swing	thousand	stone
	plaster		thing	wand	telephone
	taste			wander	
	was				
	wasn't				

Polysyllabic words for Split (see page 42)

admitted
advertise
adventure
ambulance
banana
barbeque
beautiful
bicycle
carpenter
cucumber
chimpanzee
committee
disappear
disappoint
dinosaur
dynamite
elephant
elastic
entertain
endeavour

fisherman
gardening
glimmering
hibernate
illustrate
invited
messenger
mountainous
musician
octopus
potatoes
persistant
porcupine
remember
suddenly
supervise
vibration
volcano
whispering
wonderful

but ter fly

List of words for Take one, make one (see page 44)

catch	itch	blue	city
latch	pitch	new	pity
match	which	shoe	pretty
patch	witch	who	witty
claw	bun	height	brain
door	done	knight	pane
saw	son	sight	rain
sore	sun	site	reign
go	bird	long	bang
sew	heard	song	hang
slow	stirred	strong	rang
snow	third	wrong	sprang

Possible words for Think and link (see page 45)

ARE	ONE	OUGH	ATCH	EAD	MB
are	alone	although	catch	ahead	bomb
area	bone	bough	hatch	already	bomber
beware	done	cough	hatchet	bread	comb
care	gone	drought	match	dreadful	combing
glare	lonely	enough	patch	head	climb
parent	money	ought	scratch	instead	climbing
square	none	rough	watch	lead	crumb
	one	though		leader	lamb
	stone	through		read	limb
	telephone				numb
					thumb

See other word lists, eg our ear ou

These lists are also useful for King patience, see page 32.

Think and link grid (see page 45)

Criss-cross and Word Search grids (see pages 58 and 63)

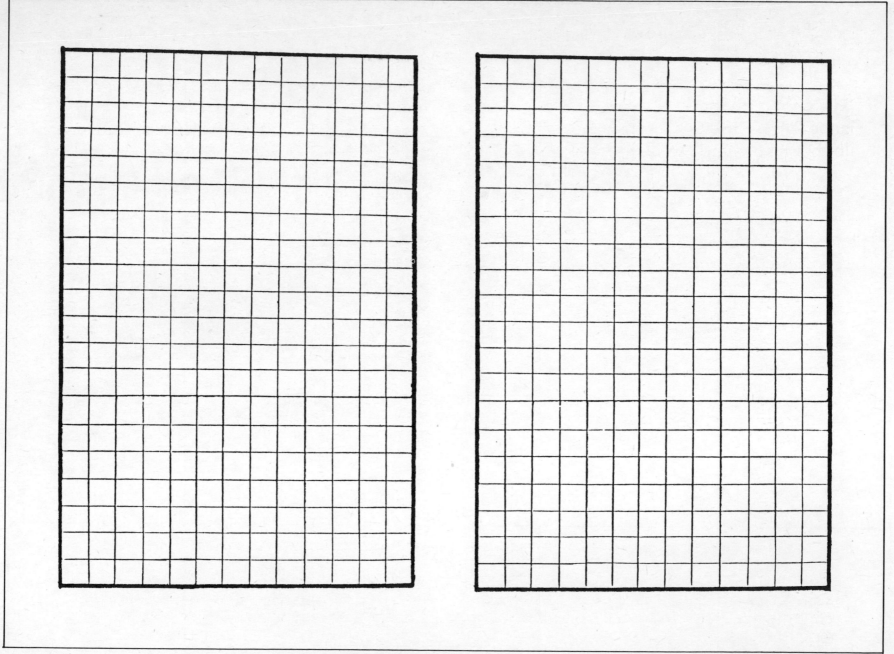

Attack-a-track (see page 66)

abcdefghijklmnopqrstuvwxyz

1   cran pob spitnec ibande 5 wysf myg nubboh
    jklm ojpr. Nopqr dur okym vtwolb yaln hmu
    ixnpe wnot. Stipqo guprum seng zaback
    ilbober zuml irvep mywl igpux ryk izplak.

2   Stibl am crin abco stod rand. Stogon par dolg
    stirm. Plend oolm wtox spirlg emperf. Rihg
    smoll shimu klast brilg inepm borl. Soppek
    narj ghax. Fonr trilk smilt prof sta rimt stnog.
    Flyt opral impoln redk. Proj sequet imsit
    orsem lewt. Coyz wixen dyelk suay slyt yloum.
    Struve lang swial dexloy pling ynasen arzgel.

3   Stalc orb pneot sin nsuen. Conlan edo peylon
    onfil tu. Ghostu sgin joyn bolk. Spolt paim
    ungn. Nadub abooc strup fottu. Quaple imtu
    semu tribbol. Bo manru porsut imtu. Vunpu
    vowti cruz almty zazu. Raxen tym blyxen
    dizom.

4   Alcam roy liber si vons stelb. Kred aget ghix
    flento rah. Oxick preulib soll awocey prilk.
    Slont haj benk golab sofgom shulm. Recarrj si
    gaje sokli parx. Dwmam spolond po klup rah
    selguare. Wims govem chek noos aaxlno
    woa putee. Con tamu olivwo son tixiw gerg
    hysizl.

ABCDEFGHIJKLMNOPQRSTUVWXYZ

1   ABER BLICK WAN MRN. CRUB. DIN OLSO
    FLIT E R FLOGUM UP GAR ET HAR PART. IN
    INFLOT UND ABER BLICK VON JSPNU.
    KINT FLOT LISP VON KNUT SED IT FLU
    TUMB. MR N P SUT GUNT-ORB. PTRU EPN
    QUIRT REXUM SFLT UB DISH ROST. SID
    TING ET PNU U U CRUB PND ND PPR IST
    DIN FOT VLIOT LOS MR WIHS EP FORT X Y
    ZYGINT.

2   CRBAT SO LABT NAK RICCK DOM TAHI
    SEJO CYMOT. LIK GAGON OFLT SOOGN
    SHOHEC NA ROTSH MI TOLAG KAVA
    RANIJ SRALOBOT. TE ONEL SKLIN OOEB
    SA ORINT BLIQUE IMART UNN RSOT
    LRINO. STLUP SELQUI NURT OSGN STNOT
    CRULT OVWI STUXN BLOY ABBO COZIN.

Alphabet maze – Upper case (see page 67)

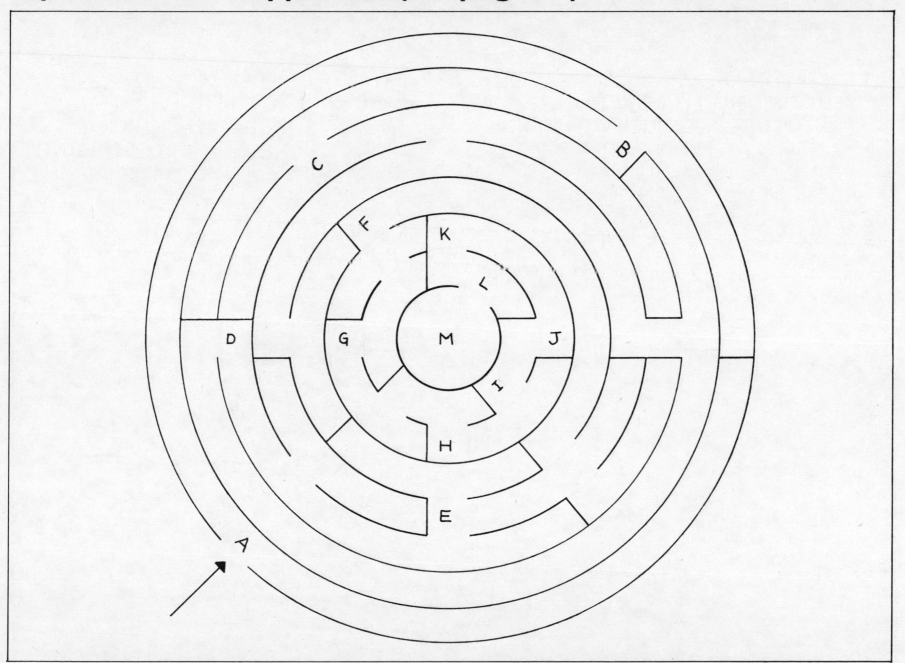

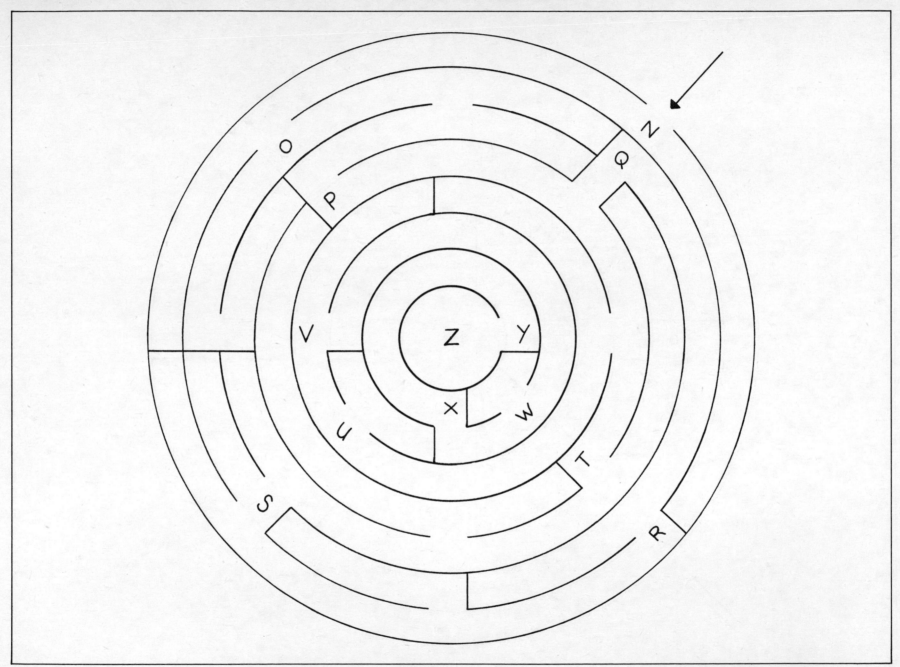

Alphabet maze – Lower case (see page 67)

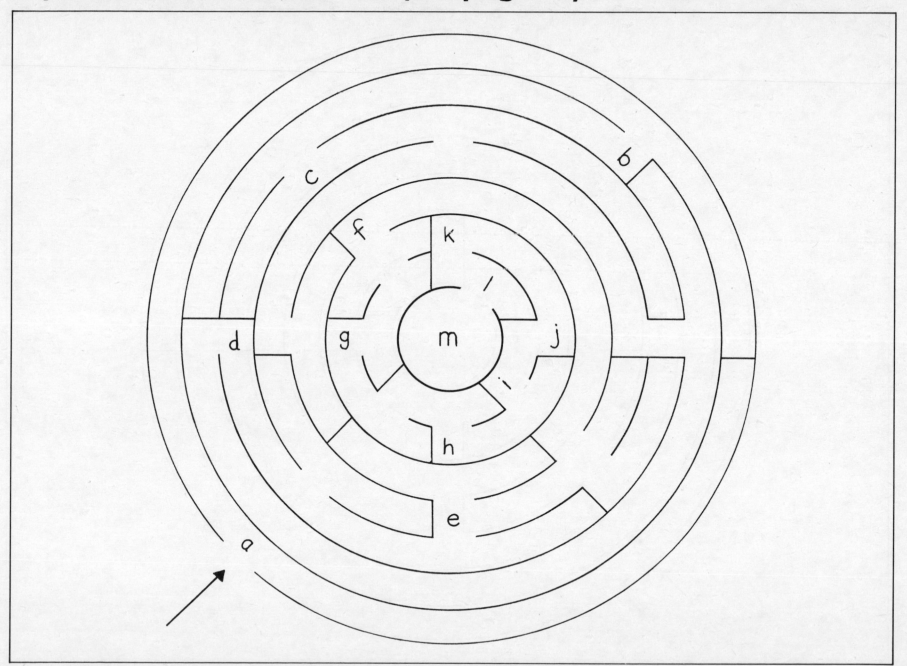

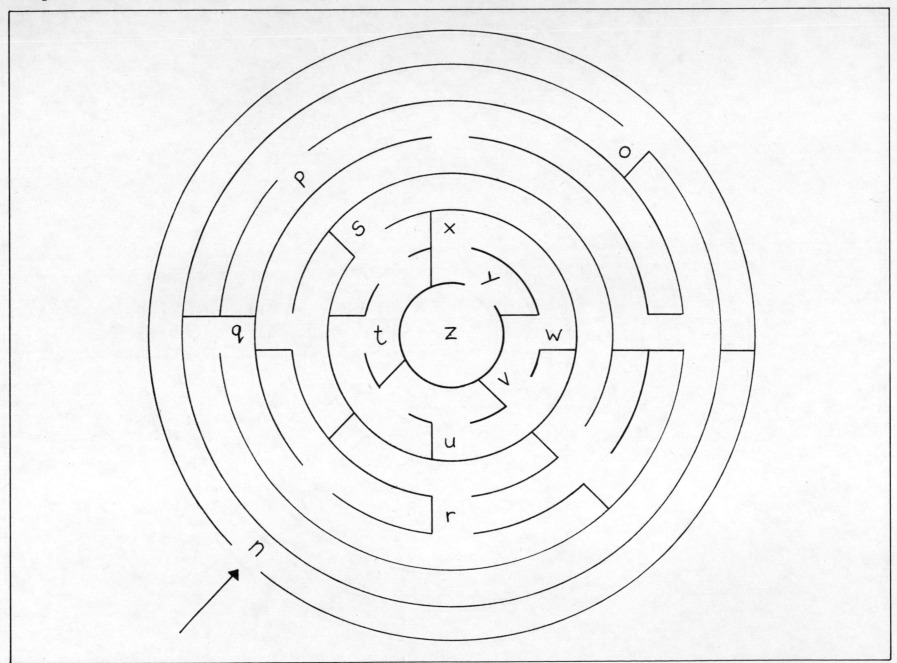

Spinners

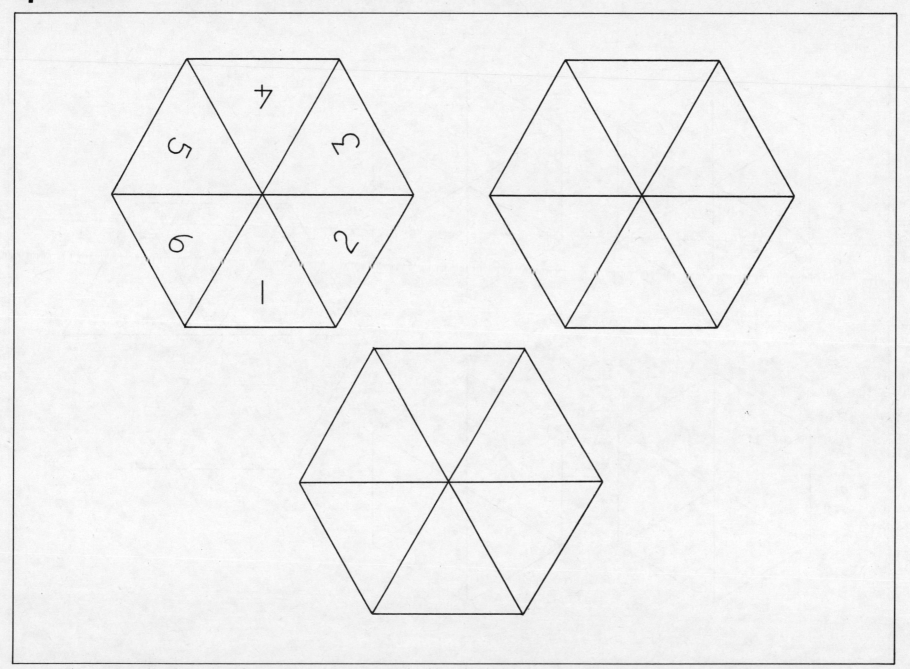

Spinners

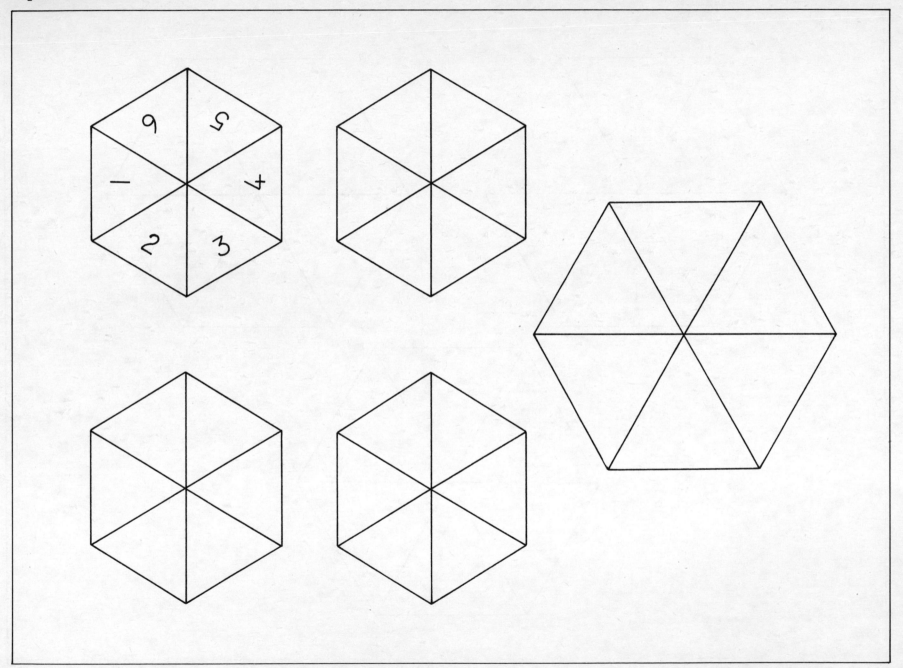

Useful letter-strings

oes	ie	ear	our	ough	igh
does	belief	appear	course	although	bright
doesn't	believe	dear	court	bough	delight
echoes	cashier	earl	favourite	bought	fight
goes	chief	early	fourteen	cough	flight
heroes	field	earn	flour	enough	fright
mosquitoes	fierce	earth	hour	fought	high
potatoes	frieze	fear	journey	ought	knight
shoes	frontier	hear	pour	rough	light
toes	grief	heard	sour	thought	might
tomatoes	grieve	heart	tour	through	night
torpedoes	lie	learn	your	tough	right
volcanoes	niece	pear			sight
	pie	pearl			tight
	piece	rear			
	priest	rehearse			
	relief	research			
	shield	search			
	siege	wear			
	thief				
	yield				

Final blends

nd
and
band
brand
hand
sand
stand
strand
end
bend
lend
spend
tend
find
kind
mind
rind
wind
blond
bond
fond
pond
fund

nk
bank
hank
rank
stank
tank
thank
yank
ink
blink
brink
clink
drink
link
pink
rink
sink
stink
think
wind
bonk
honk
monk
bunk
chink
junk
sunk

nt
ant
chant
elephant
infant
plant
bent
confident
dent
lent
spent
tent
flint
hint
lint
mint
sprint
squint
stint
tint

mp

camp
champ
clamp
damp
lamp
ramp
stamp
tramp
crimp
imp
limp
scrimp
pomp
romp
stomp
bump
chump
dump
frump
hump
lump
plump
rump
stump

st

cast	
fast	
last	
mast	
vast	
best	
chest	
crest	
guest	
jest	
nest	
pest	
quest	
rest	
test	
vest	
west	
fist	post
mist	bust
optimist	crust
wrist	dust
lost	gust
frost	August
most	just
	must
	rust

ou
house
mouse
found
round
ground
mouth
colour
loud
cloud
flour
shout
pound
sound
cousin
country
soup
trouble
double
scout
couple
mountain
trousers

ue
blue
true
rescue
cruel
tissues
tongue
Tuesday
avenue
glue
sue
value
issue
clue
cue
due
hue

pp
slippers
clapping
trapped
skipping
supper
shopping
happy
puppy
stopped
appear

dd
muddle
puddle
skidded
saddle
address
suddenly
ladder
pudding
wedding
adding

A check list of do's and don'ts with spelling (see page 15)

Do
- Talk to your child's teacher/school about spelling and how they approach it.

- Encourage them to play word games eg KAN-U-GO, BOGGLE, JUNIOR SCRABBLE, SCRABBLE AND KEYWORD, LEXICON etc.

- If your child asks for a spelling try to WRITE it down for them. Let them look at it without writing and then take it away and see if they can write it from memory. Finally let them check yours against theirs. Of course most children ask just as you have put your hands in water — resist the temptation give the letters and tell them to leave a space. Later write it down and go through the procedure as outlined above.

- Encourage your child to take an interest in words and to look closely at them. See if they can find words within words eg Which four words can they find in MOTHER without changing the letter order.

- Remember that spelling is developmental. Don't expect your child to run before she can walk.

- Encourage your child to write for you — shopping lists, holiday plans, telephone messages, thank-you letters etc, and praise and help him or her with this.

- Remember spelling and handwriting are not indicators of intelligence.

- Encourage your child to check his or her own work. Often 'reading it backwards' helps as then the meaning does not interfere with the spelling.

- Do remember that spelling is a very different skill from reading — a child who is a good reader is not necessarily a good speller, nor are they being lazy. Ask your school how to help.

- Give your child help when he is using a dictionary, eg write down the first three letters of the word they want and then let them find the word. See if a 'Speller's Dictionary' would be useful for them.

Don't

● Don't tell your child he is a bad speller. Children who believe they are poor generally become poorer.

● Don't call out the letters when the child wants a spelling.

● Don't tell your child if you were a poor speller! They begin to believe it is not worth trying as they have obviously inherited your weaknesses.

● Don't give your child a list of words to learn unless you know they are words she wants; then consider how she should learn them.

● NEVER sound out a word. Phonics will soon become unreliable eg said, make. This just undermines the child's confidence.

● Never criticise your child's written effort with regard to spelling. You will end up with a reluctant writer.

● Don't say 'use a dictionary' to a child wanting to know a spelling. A dictionary is not easy to use if you do not know what you are looking for. Dictionaries are more useful for meanings than spelling.

Alphabet and picture cards

Picturecards

Picturecards

113

Picturecards

Picturecards

Alphabet – upper case

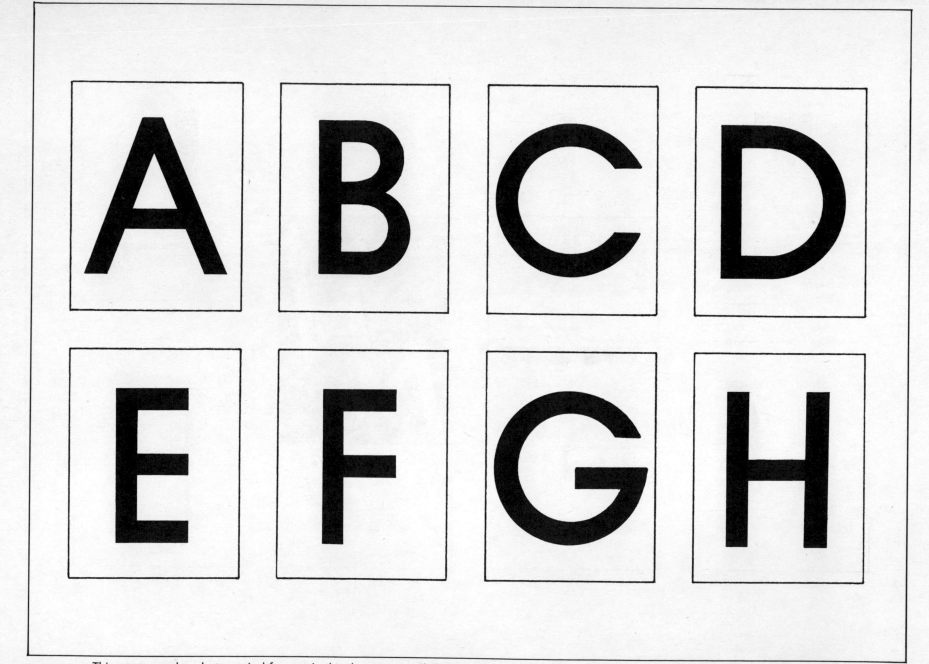

Alphabet – upper case

Alphabet – upper case

Alphabet – upper case

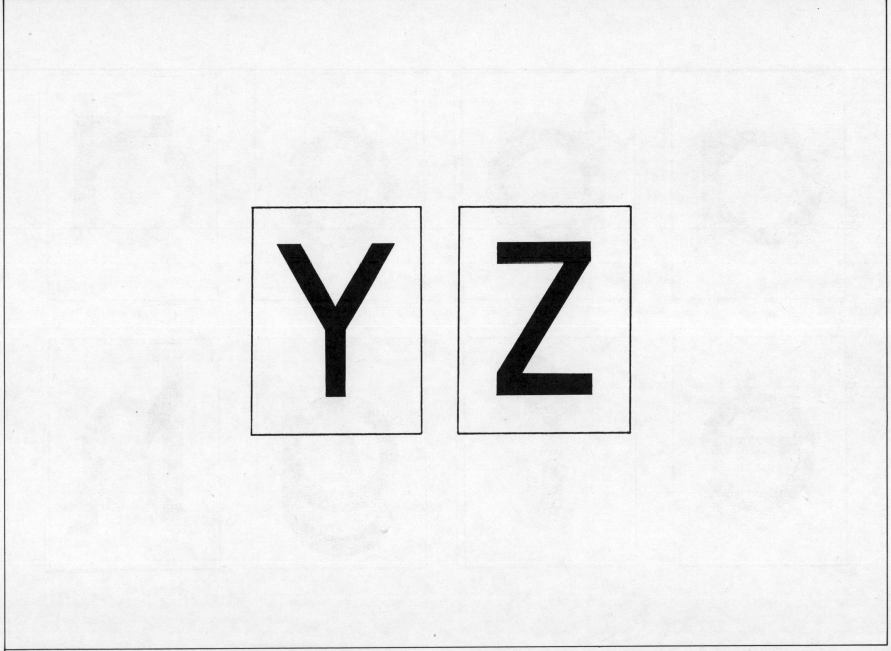

Alphabet – lower case

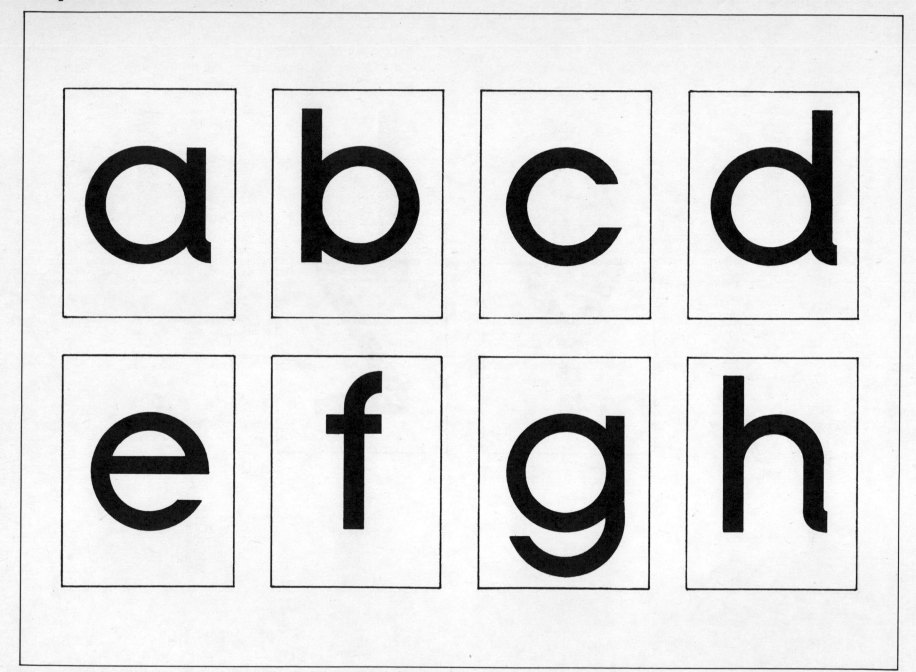

Alphabet – lower case

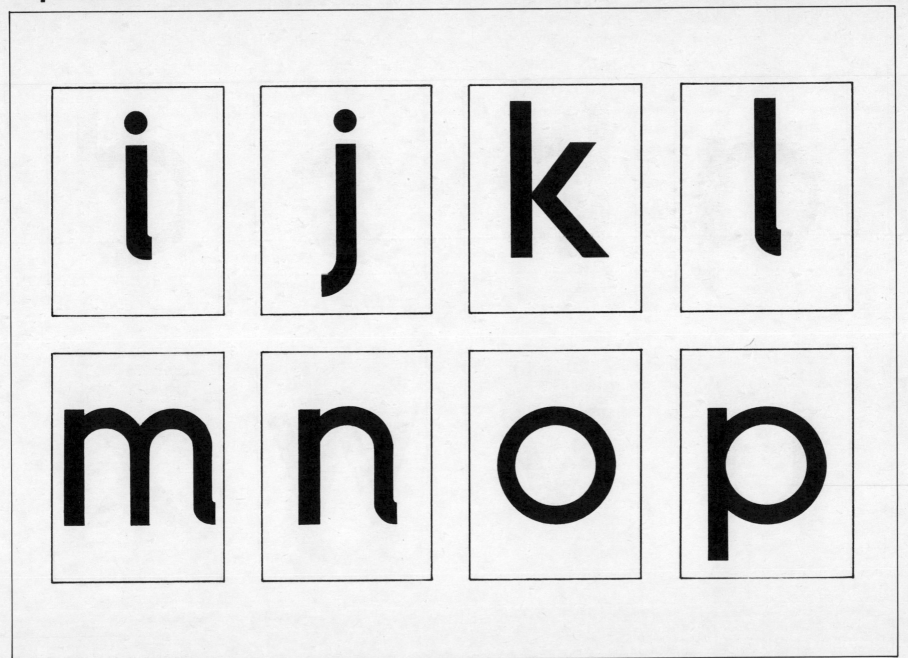

Alphabet – lower case

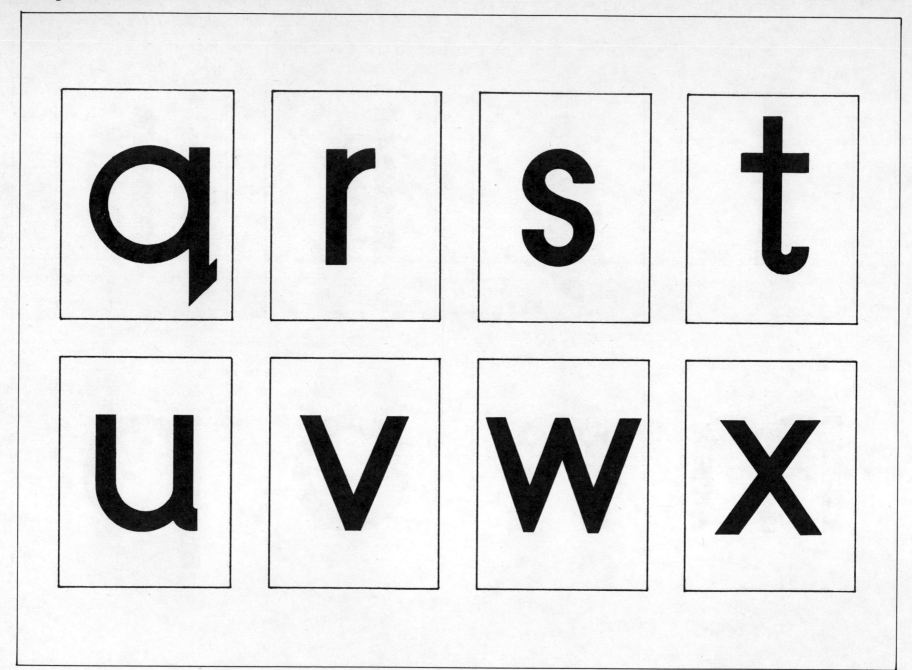

Alphabet – lower case

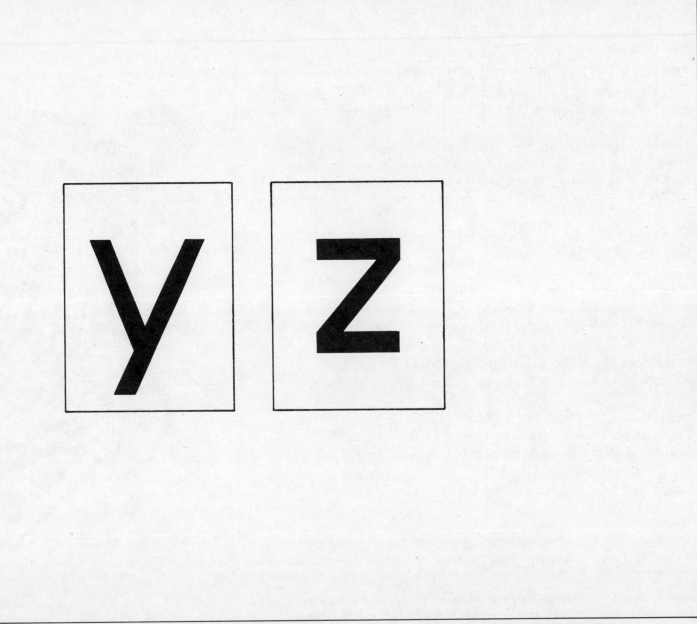

Book references

The Reading Teacher Vol 39 No 2 (1985) 'The Development of Spelling Ability and Linguistic Strategies' K F Anderson.

Developmental Medicine and Child Neurology Vol 23 (1981) 'The Organisation of Motor Patterns for Spelling: an Effective Remedial Strategy for Backward Readers' L Bradley.

Children's Reading Problems P Bryant and L Bradley (Blackwell 1985).

A Language for Life A A Bullock (DES 1975).

What Did I Write M Clay (Heinemann 1975).

Hip Pocket Spelling C Cripps (Harcourt, Brace & Janovich).

Remedial Education Vol 18 No 1 (1983) 'A Report of an Experiment to See Whether Young Children Can Be Taught to Write from Memory' C Cripps.

Cognitive Process in Spelling Ed Frita Uta (Academic Press 1980).

The Reading Teacher Vol 34 No 4 (1981) 'Learning to Spell Developmentally' J R Gentry.

The Reading Teacher Vol 36 No 2 (1982) 'An Analysis of Developmental Spelling in GYNX AT WORK' J R Gentry.

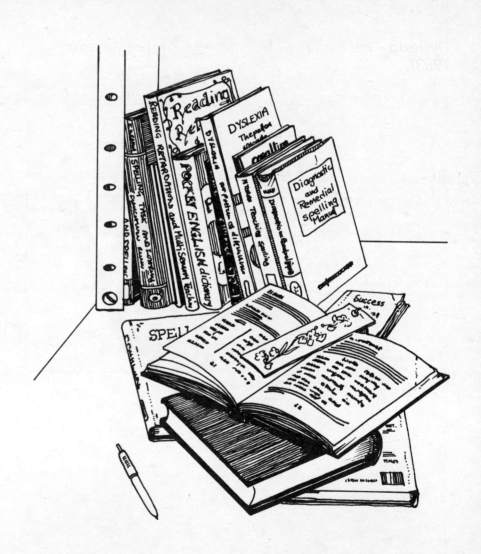

Alpha to Omega B Hornsby and Shear (Heinemann 1974).

Reading Retardation and Multi-Sensory Teaching C Hulme (Routledge, Keegan & Paul 1987).

Dyslexia – the Pattern of Difficulties T R Miles (Granada 1983).

Individualised Spelling Assignments (NARE 1983).

Aston Index M Newton (Learning Development Aids).

Success in Spelling M Peters (Cambridge Institute of Education 1970).

Spelling Caught or Taught M Peters (Routledge, Keegan & Paul 1967 and 1985).

Diagnostic & Remedial Spelling Manual M Peters (Macmillan 1979).

Teaching Spelling M Torbe (Ward Lock Educational 1977).

Spelling Task & Learning B Wade and K Wedell (Educational Review 1976).

Acknowledgements

The publishers gratefully acknowledge permission from the following sources to reproduce copyrighted material: Spike Milligan Productions Ltd for 'The ABC' poem and Methuen Children's Books Ltd for the extract from *Winnie the Pooh* by A A Milne (Magnet Edition, 1982).

Every effort has been made to trace and acknowledge contributions. If any right has been omitted the publishers offer their apologies and will rectify this in subsequent editions following notification.

The authors wish to thank all the children and schools who helped to play and improve all the activities and games in this book.

Other Bright Ideas titles

Previous titles in this series available are:

Bright Ideas Seasonal Activities
0 590 70831 7   £5.45

Bright Ideas Language Development
0 590 70834 1   £5.45

Bright Ideas Science
0 590 70833 3   £5.45

Bright Ideas Christmas Art and Craft
0 590 70832 5   £5.45

Bright Ideas Reading Activities
0 590 70535 0   £5.45

Bright Ideas Maths Activities
0 590 70534 2   £5.45

More Bright Ideas Christmas Art and Craft
0 590 70601 2   £5.45

Bright Ideas Classroom Management
0 590 70602 0   £5.45

Bright Ideas Games for PE
0 590 70690 X   £5.45

Bright Ideas Crafty Moneymakers
0 590 70689 6   £5.45

Bright Ideas Music
0 590 70700 0   £5.45

Bright Ideas Assemblies
0 590 70693 4   £5.45

Bright Ideas Writing
0 590 70701 9   £5.45

Bright Ideas Lifesavers
0 590 70694 2   £5.45

Bright Ideas Christmas Activities
0 590 70803 1   £5.45

Bright Ideas History
0 590 70804 X   £5.45

Set of any six titles   £27

Write to Scholastic Publications Ltd, Westfield Road, Southam, Leamington Spa, Warwickshire CV33 0JH. Enclose your remittance. Make cheques payable to Scholastic Publications Ltd.

'It is a pity that Chawcer who had such genyus was so
unedicated. He's the wuss speller I know of.'
Artemus Ward, *At the Tomb of Shakespeare* 1822.